ECOMMERCE AND DROPSHIPPING

Step By Step Guide To Scaling Success And Achieving Financial Freedom

HENRY STANLEY

Copyright © 2019

All rights reserved

All rights to this book are reserved. No permission is given for any part of this book to be reproduced, transmitted in any form or means; electronic or mechanical, stored in a retrieval system, photocopied, recorded, scanned, or otherwise. Any of these actions require the proper written permission of the publisher.

ECOMMERCE AND DROPSHIPPING

DISCLAIMER	**9**
INTRODUCTION	**10**
PART ONE	**13**
CREATING FORTUNE WITH E-COMMERCE	**13**
CHAPTER ONE	**14**
UNDERSTANDING E-COMMERCE	**14**
WHAT IS E-COMMERCE?	**14**
WHY YOU SHOULD ENGAGE IN E-COMMERCE AS AN ENTREPRENEUR	18
CHAPTER TWO	**23**
TYPES OF E-COMMERCE	**23**
CHAPTER THREE	**29**
BUILDING AN E-COMMERCE BUSINESS: STEP BY STEP	**29**

CHAPTER FOUR — 33

STEP 1: RESEARCHING THE FUNDAMENTALS OF E-COMMERCE — 33

The E-commerce Revenue Models — 36

CHAPTER FIVE — 41

STEP 2: E-COMMERCE NICHE RESEARCH — 41

CHAPTER SIX — 48

STEP 3: SELECTING PERSONAS AND YOUR PRODUCTS — 48

CHAPTER SEVEN — 55

STEP 4: CREATE YOUR BUSINESS AND BRAND — 55

CHAPTER EIGHT — 65

STEP 5: CREATING YOUR ONLINE STORE — 65

CHAPTER NINE — 74

STEP 6: BRINGING CUSTOMERS TO YOUR STORE — 74

CHAPTER TEN — 80

STEP 7: CARRYING OUT MARKETING STRATEGIES FOR YOUR PRODUCTS ONLINE — 80

CHAPTER ELEVEN — 85

E-COMMERCE TOOLS FOR STARTUPS — 85

CHAPTER TWELVE — 95

CHALLENGES FACING E-COMMERCE — 95

CHAPTER THIRTEEN — 103

AVOIDING E-COMMERCE MISTAKES — 103

PART TWO — 111

AMASSING WEALTH WITH THE DROPSHIPPING MODEL 111

CHAPTER FOURTEEN 112

GETTING TO KNOW DROPSHIPPING 112

WHY YOU SHOULD ENGAGE IN DROPSHIPPING 114

CHAPTER FIFTEEN 123

IS DROPSHIPPING FOR YOU? 123

CHAPTER SIXTEEN 130

HOW TO START DROPSHIPPING 130

CHAPTER SEVENTEEN 136

SELECTING THE BEST PRODUCT 136

HOW YOU CAN FIND THE RIGHT PRODUCT FOR DROPSHIPPING 140

CHAPTER EIGHTEEN — 142

UNDERSTANDING YOUR MARKET — 142

FACTORS YOU SHOULD CONSIDER ABOUT YOUR TARGET MARKET — 146

CHAPTER NINETEEN — 148

IDENTIFY THE BEST SUPPLIERS — 148

SEARCHING FOR A SUPPLIER — 151

CHAPTER TWENTY — 155

GROW YOUR DROPSHIPPING BUSINESS — 155

CHAPTER TWENTY-ONE — 165

DEALING WITH DROPSHIPPING MISTAKES — 165

CHAPTER TWENTY-TWO — 173

DEALING WITH DROPSHIPPING CHALLENGES	**173**
PART THREE	**179**
PROVIDING NEEDFUL ANSWERS	**179**
CHAPTER TWENTY-THREE	**180**
QUESTIONS ON E-COMMERCE	**180**
CHAPTER TWENTY- FOUR	**185**
QUESTIONS ON DROPSHIPPING	**185**
CONCLUSION	**192**
THE FUTURE OF DROP SHIPPING AND YOU	**192**

Disclaimer

All knowledge contained in this book is given for informational and educational purposes only. The author is not in any way accountable for any results or outcomes that emanate from using this material. Constructive attempts have been made to provide information that is both accurate and effective, but the author is not bound for the accuracy or use/misuse of this information.

INTRODUCTION

The poke-nosing attitude of technology has spread its reach into the retailing business. The result of this is the creation of a virtual world that grosses in billions of dollars for those who are ready to take up the opportunity. Online retailing is a go-to form of retailing that distinguishes itself from conventional physical retailing. With an investment lesser than what is required to own a physical store, you can set up a wider store online that can cater to the need of people. Also, more than the geographical limitations you will experience with your physical retailing business, online retailing offers a global presence, where you can have access to the demands of people from all over the world.

E-commerce is a promising business model that brings money from different parts of the world to a person without limitations. All you need to do is to create a space for yourself on the internet and let people see what you sell. They are willing to buy, once they see what they need. The selling point of e-commerce business lies in the fact that the customers can sit back in the comfort of their homes or offices and make orders of whatever they need using their smartphones and laptop.

The general acceptance of the e-commerce business has different birth models, of which the dropship model is one important aspect that is making a wave. Just imagine you starting a business worth millions of dollars, with just a few hundreds of dollars. It is really possible with dropshipping. You have products worth million in your cart, and you can sell while you make your profit. Yet, it gives you less risk.

This book is geared toward helping you create a fortune from e-commerce and dropshipping in particular. You will be having an in-depth insight into what e-commerce and dropshipping are all about. You will get to know how to start the business, with a step-by-step guide that will help you start the business successfully. More than these, you will be having ample information about the certain challenges you are likely to encounter, and the mistakes that are likely to occur. Don't panic because I have provided the answers to each of them to aid you. E-commerce and drop shipping is a great business that you can invest your time and resources to create a great fortune. It is simply you utilizing the benefits of technology to your advantage and creating an EMPIRE OF WEALTH.

PART ONE

CREATING FORTUNE

WITH E-COMMERCE

CHAPTER ONE

UNDERSTANDING E-COMMERCE

WHAT IS E-COMMERCE?

E-commerce is a system of business that involves buying and selling of goods and services using electronic means; this is why some call it electronic commerce. E-commerce involves the transaction of business over the internet. It is one of the novel experiences that technological advancement has brought into our world from the angle of the economy. E-commerce involves all forms of businesses, as long as money is involved, in transaction form, it is e-commerce. There are different transactions going on the internet these days. Some of such transactions are a transfer of funds, money, data, and goods. It is even possible for services to be rendered via the internet. When all these occur, e-commerce is ongoing. E-commerce, in a nutshell, refers to a virtual transaction between two or more people. There are lots of businesses that are making high revenue by selling and rendering services on the internet. Some of these companies include Flipkart, Shopify, Amazon, eBay, Jumia, Olx, among others. With the present rating of the e-commerce market, there is an expectation of $27 trillion by the year 2020 from the e-commerce market. This is to show in simple terms the strength of the market, how popular it has become.

E-commerce involves a virtual market space where buyers and sellers meet to transact. For example, you log into your Amazon and buy a book. Amazon is the marketplace, while the author of the book is the seller, and you are the buyer. Unlike the conventional means of buying and selling, where you will walk into a bookstore, and pick a book you want, while you pay in cash to the seller, e-commerce gives the opportunity to be in the comfort of your home while you surf the internet to pick up anything you want or need. You make the payment online, and if there is a need for Amazon to deliver the book, you would state this, and it will be brought to you. E-commerce is a fast-growing business in the global economy. E-commerce enables you, as the seller, to sell globally without hindrances. You do not need any physical shop. People only need to visit your website and demand whatever product they need, and you do the needful by sending it over to them.

HISTORY OF E-COMMERCE

The history of what is presently known and called e-commerce today started from the introduction of computers, modems, and the internet. The introduction of the internet for commercial use in 1991 is instrumental to the coming of electronic commerce that connects sellers and buyers alike. The commercialization of the internet paved the way for many businesses to find a place for themselves on the internet by setting up their websites.

At the start of e-commerce, EDI, which is Electronic Data Interchange and EFT, which is Electronic Funds Transfer serve as the means of executing transaction online. These were the tools that sellers and buyers used to carry out their transactions. Four years later, new security protocols such as HTTP, and DSL were developed, and they made it possible for businesses and every other person using the internet to have faster access to the internet.

By the year 2000, many businesses already have their presence on the internet, and they were busy carrying out trading activities with buyers. People started buying goods from companies, through secure connections, and by paying electronically. There was a persistent increase in the growth of e-commerce as the years went by. 3.4% of the total sales made in 2007 came from e-commerce. The advantages of e-commerce over the store and mail order method was the main factor driving its growth. The fact that a buyer does not have to leave his or her house and will still have access to whatever product he or she desires, while the product will be delivered to his or her doorstep were very crucial in making many people opt to form the electronic commerce.

The History of e-commerce is well expounded with the formation of Amazon and eBay. They were part of the businesses that gave room for transacting online. These two businesses are among the five largest e-commerce retailers in the world. They share the rank with other businesses such as Dell, Hewlett Packard, Office Depot, and Staples. The commonest products on e-commerce are books, computers, music, office equipment, and electronics. The history of e-commerce tells us more about a new world that is filled with development and keeps revolving in a way that considers the benefits of the consumers.

Why You Should Engage in E-commerce as an Entrepreneur

I have been confronted many times with questions by many young entrepreneurs on why they should take their businesses online. One of such once asked me: "Why should I create a website and start displaying my products?" the answer to that question lies in understanding the benefits of e-commerce for you and your business.

To Expand Globally: one of the reasons you need to place your business on the internet and go into e-commerce is because it will make you go global. Whatever product you are selling or service you render, don't you think there are other people outside the United States in need of it? You can reach them by placing your product within their reach with is only possible through the internet because the internet has made the whole world a small place. Your store will limit to a specific geographical area. If, for instance, you have your store in California, and you wish to expand to New Jersey, you would have to open another store in New Jersey. However, when you place your place on the internet, you only need a store in California, from which you can send your goods to people around the country and beyond.

Consistent Availability: unlike your physical store that you have to close at a particular hour of the day, your online store will always be opened to the world. Customers can always wake up in the middle of the night and decide to order for a particular product, which means even while you sleep, you are making a fortune. Your store online is always opened regardless of the time of the day.

ECOMMERCE AND DROPSHIPPING

You Spend Less: can you imagine making more money by spending less? Yes, you can make it. When you compare the cost of running an online store with a physical store, you would see that there is a wide range of differences between the two. Your online store does not require a rent payment, you have no cleaners, and less number of staff to pay, and you will spend little in your operating cost. E-commerce offers you the possibility of spending less and making more, while you deliver more to your customers at a high level of satisfaction.

Ease of Managing Inventory: the process of managing your inventory in an online store is easier. Every inventory is carefully analyzed automatically. There are online tools and third-party vendors that help to play the role. With this, online businesses are able to save more by not spending much on operations and inventory. There has also been persistent growth in the management of inventory. There are observable sophistications with the tools that are used to monitor the inventory. It is possible for you to sell and monitor your stock in your store or on other market platforms such as eBay, Amazon, etc.

It Gives room for Laser-Focused Marketing: Laser-focused marketing permits you to select the specific category of customers you want to offer your goods to. With e-commerce, businesses can now gather data of consumers to identify the right people they want for their products. With Laser-focused marketing, there is a lower expense on customer acquisition, and the business will remain agile. One of the possibilities of laser-focused marketing is that you can target males between the age of 25 and 40 that live in urban areas for your product. With the marketing focus, there will be specific people that will have access to the product. You cannot do this in your physical store.

It Ensures a High Return on Investment: most of the e-commerce businesses enjoy high profitability. Since they spend less on their operations, and they are able to target their real customers, coupled with the fact that they are not limited in their reach, they make more money, but spend less, and that equals high profit.

You Enjoy Location Independence: your business online does not thrive with any location. You are not tied down to a specific location or geography. All you need is a laptop and internet connection always to stay online to approve orders and make preparation to deliver them. There is no fear of location or the need to carry out location research before you start the business.

CHAPTER TWO

TYPES OF E-COMMERCE

E-commerce has various forms it comes in. There are basically two categorizations of all these forms. You can either categorize it based on products or services it offers, or the buyers the seller is transacting with, and the platforms on which the business is done. E-commerce is a large business platform. It is quite larger than you may think. The internet is a broad space that tries to connect and contract the world into a small space. You need to understand the possible forms in which your online business can come in and understand the one that you engage in as you make the decision to bring your business online.

Classification Based on Product and Services

Stores that sell goods

Some e-commerce businesses are online retailers that sell physical goods for consumption or use. Some of such stores include homeware stores, apparel stores, gift stores, electronic stores, etc. these stores present their items online and give their prospective customers the opportunity to search for the particular item they need and add the item to their virtual shopping cart, which they will get after completing the transaction. When you complete the order, the store makes arrangements to ship the item to you. There are many retail stores online. Some of them are Bonobos, a men's wear retail store, Zappos, a shoe retail store, etc.

Service Providers

Just like goods, you can also buy and sell services online. We have educators, consultants, and freelancers online who render their services to those that require it. There are different means of buying the service of people online. For some, you are permitted to buy the services rendered outright; an example is what happens on freelance sites such as Upwork, and Fiverr. On any of these two sites, a buyer is required to place an order before the seller provides the service. For some service providers, you need to meet them. You only get to connect with them online, but the service will be rendered when you meet them physically.

Digital Products Sellers

The concept of e-commerce itself supports digital activities more than physical activities. Hence, there are many electronic goods that are sold on the e-commerce market. The digital products are not tangible. They include eBooks, graphics, online courses, software, pictures, games, and many more. There are many popular businesses that sell e-product online such as Udemy, which offers a wide variety of online courses, Shutterstock, which sells various kinds of stock pictures, Slack, which sells real-time messaging, archiving, and search for teams.

E-commerce has another categorization based on the parties involved. This form of e-commerce is the commonest. This categorization is based on the participants involved in the business. Below are the different forms of e-commerce based on this category:

Business to consumers (B2C): As the name implies, the business is carried out between the company and the direct users of the products. The consumers, most times, browse the internet and seek products that will suit their taste. Each time they make this move, they try to check out the description of the product they want to buy, look for reviews on the products, and these pick the product they actually want before they place their order. It is the company's duty to ship the item down to the consumer. Amazon, Alibaba, Jabong, among others, are popular examples of business in this category of e-commerce.

Business to Business (B2B): This form involves a business transaction that goes on between two businesses without the final consumers. It often occurs between the company, which is also the manufacturer and the wholesaler or retailer. A business that transacts with another business is on the B2B model of e-commerce. Examples of such businesses are ADP, a company that processes the payroll of workers, Square, which is a company that offers payment solutions to SMBs, and many others.

Consumer to Business (C2B): The C2B is directly opposite to the B2C e-commerce business. This involves the consumer offering a company service or good. It is possible for a consumer to develop software and sell it to a company. When the final consumer contributes in terms of money to a business, also, it is considered C2B. Most of the crowdsourcing campaigns are part of C2B e-commerce. One of the most popular businesses that are running C2B e-commerce is Soma. Soma deals with the water filters that are eco-friendly. In 2012, the company launched a Kickstarter campaign for funding the production of its products. They were able to raise $147,444 from the campaign.

Consumer to consumer (C2C): From its name, it involves the retailing of a product by a consumer to another consumer. This is a common phenomenon online. People decide to sell their used items to another person, which they may later use the money earned to buy another product or use it for other pressing matters. The common items sold by consumers are cars, bikes, phones, and other electronic items. Among the popular online platforms where the C2C e-commerce takes place are, OLX, eBay, Quikr, etc.

Government to Business (G2B): This form of business occurs when a company pays for certain goods of the government, or services online. For example, when a business pays tax online.

Business to Government (B2G): It is also possible to have a business transaction between a company and the government. For instance, if a government agency or sector buys from a company online, B2G has occured. Also, it is possible for an agency of the government to hire a company such as a design company to help with the updating of its website. This is also a form of B2G. Construction companies that are hired to carry out major government projects can also pay via the internet, and all this also will count as B2G.

Consumer to Government (C2G): It is possible for the consumers to have a transaction with the government directly. Example of such transaction is the payment of toll fee, traffic ticket, or car registration renewals, which are often carried out online. These are C2G e-commerce transactions.

CHAPTER THREE

BUILDING AN E-COMMERCE BUSINESS: STEP BY STEP

E-commerce business has come to stay, no doubt. The question one is now left with is how does a person start the business from scratch so as to enjoy the benefits that it has to offer? For me, I have always enjoyed helping others acquire knowledge about what will be beneficial to them. In this chapter and subsequent ones, I will be doing just that again by taking you through the certain activities you need to engage in to build your e-commerce business. One thing I have observed is that when entrepreneurs are not well-informed, they will have challenges in their business. There many young starters out there struggling with the e-commerce business because they do not have ample information that will set them on the right track and fasten their process of growth. My target is to make sure that you have a great sail with me in the process of investing and running your e-commerce business.

Just like every other business, e-commerce business has a lot to offer you when you engage in it rightly. There has been consistency in the growth of the business, and this is one reason I will be encouraging any willing investor not to stay away from it. There are possibilities of complications; however, when it is carefully run, the business has more advantages to give than the disadvantages. Selling online is a different thing entirely. If you have a physical store, and you think the knowledge is more than enough for you to work online, you can never be more wrong. The model to follow online for your business is quite different from what is obtainable in the real world. An e-commerce business involves all of the following: having a niche and persona; you don't focus on products, enjoying high-profit margin than you could have ever thought, you can reinvest by using the sales you get from affiliate marketing, you can easily identify the item selling best and you use the opportunity to launch new lines, and finally, there is a natural growth projection for the business.

The running of your e-commerce business is beyond the level of creating a brand name, having your products list, and starting to make sales online. It is not all about having more than enough items to show your buyers online. One important thing is how you are able to drive traffic of buyers to your site. Your attention should be on this. Your prospective customers need to leave wherever they are to log into your website and start surfing for the products they want. With a lot of competitions in the market today, how do you want to ensure that your site is visited and that you make your sale? You can only do this when you have a full understanding of how the business works. Starting an e-commerce business involves the following steps:

Researching the fundamentals of e-commerce

Carrying out an Ecommerce research

Making a persona and product selection

Establishing your brand and e-commerce business

Creating your online store

Bringing customers to your online stores

Carrying out marketing strategies for your products online All of these will be looked into one after the other, and at the end of the discourse on them, you would have understood the way forward on setting up your e-commerce business from scratch.

CHAPTER FOUR

STEP 1: RESEARCHING THE FUNDAMENTALS OF E-COMMERCE

The most important step to take at first is to look critically at e-commerce. Since it is a new business venture for you, you are not expected to jump at it without being well-informed. It is a new business entirely, and you need adequate information to be successful at it. Hence, the first step to take is to ask lots of questions and work around those questions. Do your basic research about the business and utilize the result you gain from the research to direct your next course of action. You should avoid starting your online business with guesses. It is an investment just like every other business; so, treat it as such. E-commerce business does not have a specific rule that states how things are to be done. The business structure is not one, and there are varying structures that work for everyone. Among the opportunities on e-commerce, digital product sales, software, physical products, and service-based offers are just some of the businesses you can enjoy online. There are more opportunities for anyone who is ready to make money online.

Your research on the basis of the e-commerce market should center around the available models in the business. This knowledge is what will aid you in the process of selecting what you want to sell. You may be interested in physical products. However, you don't have to fill your garage with products; neither do you have to place your investment in gathering products. The question is, how do you plan to manage your inventory and source your products? There are structures on the ground that will help you achieve your target with e-commerce without you losing or having to spend more. One such means for you to have a high-profit return without you investing highly on your products at the beginning is for you to embrace dropshipping.

If you are planning to set up a warehouse, you will be spending more at the start of the business, and you are basically working with a wholesaling model. You need to have an idea of the business and think about the best product you want to sell using your brand. Pay attention to production and possibly, white labeling. Aside from this, you can subscribe to curating your products or an item of your products to be delivered to customers that need them. In your research, you would come across varying forms of business models that will aid your business. There is also the single product category, which works in supplementary to affiliate marketing. This model permits a person to control the content marketing and the branding of a specific product, why the rest of your commitment will be channeled toward making sales by driving traffic to your website.

The basic research done on e-commerce should cover the types of businesses one can do online, the process of selling products online, and other business models online. In a previous chapter, I have mentioned the types of businesses in e-commerce. I will look at other business revenue models that e-commerce embraces. The process of selling online will be discussed in other steps to build your online business.

The E-commerce Revenue Models

The first area you need to research is the various type of online business models you can follow. These models are the Consumer to business (C2B), Business to business (B2B), consumer to consumer(C2C), business to consumer (B2C), among others. Afterward, your attention should be drifted toward the other models you can follow to make money by identifying the process you want to follow to source your products and manage your inventory in the online business. Some sellers love it when they produce their products themselves, while other sellers do not want to have their stores full of goods. Whichever way you so wished, there is a room for you to make your sale and make a fortune from e-commerce. Below are the models to follow to secure your products and make your money:

Utilizing Drop Shipping

Dropshipping is a form of e-commerce that permits you to set up your business with a storefront, while you get the customer's money via credit cards or PayPal. All you do is get the pay, while your suppliers do the delivery. Dropshipping does not require you to have a warehouse or a wholesale store. You do not have any business with inventory management, nor the packaging of goods. However, there is a simple challenge, if you are dealing with slow suppliers, or probably the suppliers send products that are lower in quality than what the customer demands, you will take the blame. Every review by the buyer is on you. On the popular website utilizing dropshipping is Wacky Hippo. In the next part of this book, I will look more deeply into dropshipping. For you to set up your dropshipping website, you may use Shopify or Oberoi. These software tools are inexpensive and very fast to create. The commonest method to drive traffic is through Facebook ads and the creation of a quick store. This is a model you can give consideration to while you do researches.

The wholesaling or Warehousing model

You may also decide to use the warehousing model. However, you must be ready to invest heavily. This model requires inventory management, customer order tracking, gathering information about the shipping, and investing in obtaining a warehouse space. One of the most popular businesses using the wholesaling model is DollarDays. The online business has an impressive product catalog that comprises of over 260,000 products. This model makes it possible to sell to both retailers and consumers. The warehousing model is quite big for a venture, most times, you may have to push your products to big online platforms such as Amazon, eBay, etc. to make your sales.

The Private Labeling Model

This model will work for you if you have an idea of a good marketable product, but you do not have the resources to manufacture the product yourself. You can hire a manufacturer and send the prototype of your product to the manufacturing based on demand by the customers. The manufacturing may even be in charge of shipping the product to the customer directly, or the company that will sell it. This process of production is called offsite manufacturing. This method of production is an on-demand form. It offers you the possibility of changing your suppliers whenever they fail to provide you with the quality you need.

This model does not require a huge amount of startup. And consequently, you may later set up your personal factory for production. One of the popular businesses involved in offsite manufacturing is Sourcify.

The White Labeling Model

This model is similar to the private labeling model. You are allowed to choose a product sold by another company with a white label option. You are to design the package and label, and then sell it to your customers. The white labeling model is common in the wellness and beauty industries. However, it is not easily seen in any other niches. A challenge with this model is demand. You are always left with the item you order only. Many of the companies involved in the model have a minimum production quantity, and you either sell it or have it with you. Before you buy the products, you need to be sure that there are more than demands for it.

The Subscription Model

This model works by providing customers with their demanded items at a regular or interval period. Their delivery periods are scheduled, and the businesses that are involved in this model have an income that is reliable. They can also incentivize their customers and engage them to buy more subscriptions. It is quite hard to select the right product and niches. There are a few product categories that enjoy successful subscription boxes. Some of such categories are fashion, food, health and grooming, and beauty. Aside from these businesses, there are few companies that thrive on subscription.

What I love about research is that it will give you an in-depth analysis of what a business contains, and the information gathered from it will guide on how you would invest your money and not lose. Now that you are aware of the models of e-commerce that you can embrace as a startup, you know the product options you have, the platforms you have access to, and the forms of e-commerce that you can engage in, the next step is to start looking forward to gathering more information about the business. E-commerce business does not end with you knowing what model you want to use, you need to know more, and this is what I will continue to explain further.

CHAPTER FIVE

STEP 2: E-COMMERCE NICHE RESEARCH

There are many e-commerce sites that lack focus. These sites are filled up with hundreds of products in different categories, yet there is no central focus. As a starter, you ought to avoid acting like Amazon or eBay. Focus on a specific niche to create e-commerce that you can run profitably. The knowledge you got from the research on the basics of e-commerce should guide you to make the best decision on which niche you want to focus on. As a starter, you need to be known for a specific niche. You should start by investigating successful companies that are already existing in the business. Whatever area you want to settle into should be a lucrative marketplace. How do you know a lucrative marketplace? Simply, you look out for competitions. When there is no competition in a particular niche, then there is no market in it.

However, you should also avoid an overcrowded niche as a starter so as not to be lost in the midst of the giants. If possible, stay away from any niche that involves major brands. You just need to be more specific about your decision. The more you dig deep to be specific, the less you are likely to encounter competition. While you create your niche, you may work with other businesses that share the same niche with you to promote or be an affiliate and grow your customer base.

The decision on the product to focus on often serves as a challenge to most people who have made the decision to go into e-commerce. While you carry out your research on the area you can specialize in; you should avoid overthinking but rather embrace strategy in the process of choosing. The reason you need to be very careful is that if you rush into any niche, it may be unprofitable and end up wasting your resources. To be strategic, I have identified some tips for you to identify the best niche for you in your online business.

#1 – Know the Interest of Buyers

The first thing you need to know is what the customers want. What actually interests them. The key to creating a successful business is to understand the need of the buyers. If you are setting up a physical shop, the idea of filling up your shops with varieties of goods might work; however, online, you need to strategically call the attention of buyers to your site and make them stay. The best way to make them stay is to provide them with what they really want. To set up your store with goods that people will want, you can make use of Google Keyword Planner to search for the best products. Identify the keywords that have a high volume of search online. If people are not looking for the product you want to sell, there will be no one to buy it, and if there are so many searches on the product, you will make your money.

However, you will be facing a lot of challenges. Your research should involve checking out whether people are passionate about the niche you want to settle down for. There are certain examples of products that people spend a lot of dollars to purchase all because they need to follow their passion. Those in love with golf and fishing are ready to thousands of dollars on reels, lures, clubs, rods, among others. One other way to get the interest of buyers is to identify a problem that is common to a large group of people and identify a product that solves the problem. Make the product your niche and see how your sales will be high.

#2 – Study the Competition

Having identified a niche, before you place all your eggs into the basket of that specialization, you need to carry out an analysis of the competition involved in the niche. You can start by checking out Amazon for products in a complementary relationship with the product. If it happens that Amazon already has the product, then you are about to embark on a seriously competitive business. Even if you try to compete on price, it will be an uphill battle.

Another way to study the competition is to carry out SEO research. If your niche is successful, you should be ranking first on Google result each time people search the product. However, if there are lots of competitions on the products, you will not rank first. You can make use of tools like

SimilarWeb to analyze your competition. Note that you are not trying to run away from the competition. In fact, it is a good factor to consider before you select a niche. However, you need to check if it is possible for you to sell above your competitors. If not, then you would have to keep searching.

#3 – Identify your Pricing and the Margins

The basic purpose of every business is to make a profit. If you are going into an online business, then the product margin needs to be attractive. This often serves as a difficult aspect of the business, especially in a competitive market. Avoid thin profit s you can develop your business. If you are open to little profit, your business growth will be delayed. You are likely to want to go into the business even with the full knowledge that the business will not provide you with enough money. When you have such thoughts, shove it off, and make sure the business you engage in gives you enough in return for your effort.

Basically, if your margin is lower than 20%, I advise you look elsewhere for your niche, most especially if you are interested in dropshipping. Similarly, your pricing should be beneficial. Make sure you engage in a business that is profitable, not manageable, all because you want to stay online to do business.

#4 – Obtain an Existing Online Business

Another means of choosing the right niche is to acquire an existing business online. It might be quite difficult to start from the beginning with searching for the best niche. There is a possibility that you will never find the best niche that will not be challenging. And aside from that, it can be time-consuming to identify the best niche. You may just look out for the website that is for sale. Most of such sites already built their record of sales in a specific niche. You just need to identify a business that does not require any technical knowledge to operate. One thing about such business is that it already underwent the "passion test," and the process of legitimizing it has been done. You only need to make sure that the business meets your profit goals. If you can afford to buy, you should o for buying an existing business.

The niche you choose is what determines your uniqueness, and that will go a long way in determining whether you will make your profit or not. The e-commerce market is large enough to make you the fortune you want. You only need to do the right things to get the right results. Having identified your niche, the next step is to select personas and products to sell.

CHAPTER SIX

STEP 3: SELECTING PERSONAS AND YOUR PRODUCTS

Having identified your niche, the next thing is to know the people you are selling to, who you are (that is what you want your business to stand for), what your store stands for, who your ideal customers are. These are the personas you need to define. They are part of the process of building your brand. The personas you create will be the image of your newly formed company. And when you have the ideal customers you want to deal with; the next step is to come up with the specific products you want to sell. It is often great to start with a product. That way, you would be investing less at the start, and you can make use of affiliate marketing if you want to offer more products.

For example, if you are dealing with organic seed, you can identify popular organic products on Amazon and set up the content on your site that will send traffic to those affiliate products. You will still make your profit on every click made through your link. If you are investing in a product, however, you need to carry out careful evaluation. Make an effort to see any challenges that may be attached to the product, and make sure you understand how the products work and have ready-made answers to whatever questions that may arise on the product.

The challenge of what to sell is enormous for any online entrepreneur. Because of this knowledge, I have identified certain strategies that will guide you on how to select the best product for your online store. Don't be intimidated, and don't be too excited to make a choice of what product to sell without identifying the best product for you and your business.

#Strategy 1 – Locally Scarce Items

The strength of the most successful business lies in its ability to be different. If you want your online business to grow, you need to look for products that are scarce locally. For example, during the hay days of Walmart, and many other popular retail outlets, there were a lot of items available locally. However, those who need some special items such as crafting equipment, or the hobby items they often had to go online in search of them. Around you, a similar thing is happening. Identify any particular item you observe is missing locally around you, and work on placing them on your online store. At the same time, make sure the product has a high demand before you stock it. For your business success, demand plays a crucial role. It is not like an open shop where people walk in and see items they need, even without plans, they will buy. However, for your online store, people need to search for your product, and if it is not on their minds, they may never type it in the search query.

#Strategy 2 – Nationally Scarce Items

The opposite of the locally scarce items is a nationally scarce one. You are simply widening the horizon of your product's need. Some products are basically found in some locations, while there is a need for them nationally. You can make use of this opportunity to set up your online store. If you live in Hawaii, for instance, you will have access to tropical goods, which are not available on the mainland. It is quite possible for tourists to talk about how they miss some of these goods. This shows that there is a market for the goods. You only need to place them online, and when tourists go back to their states, they can still have access to the goods by simply ordering them. In such a situation, you only need to get the goods from local vendors, producers, and get local professionals to help out with the running of the business.

#Strategy 3 – Identify products with Low Turnover

The most suitable products for your online business are those that can stay long throughout the whole year and still maintain a low turnover rate. High turnover rate products are not beneficial for your benefit. Your business needs products that can endure, such that whatever information you provide for the products will always be constant even after many years. However, you should not stay in a single place all because of low turnover. You need to consistently update your website, by placing new products, with novel descriptions, and contents that are SEO filled. You should also pay attention to consistency in your update, so you always portray the same marketing format.

#Strategy 4 – Disposable and Consumable Goods

To keep your business running effectively, you should go for products that will have a need to be sold over and over again. When your products are consumable, you only need to give the customers the best service and care at their first purchase with you. Afterward, they will surely come back for more, and your income will become steady without any form of delay. Disposable goods will always generate demand, and you only have to be ready to supply the people whenever they ask.

#Strategy 5 – Trends and Demand by People

Basically, for every business, the demand by customers determine what product one should sell. You need to look out for what is in vogue and catching many people's attention. That should be your area of interest. People will always search for whatever is trending, and if you have it available, they will troop in to purchase.

#Strategy 6 – Check Out the Profit Margin

You should go for a particular product based on the profit margin it has. There are certain products, such as accessories, which you can get at a cheap rate. However, you would sell at a higher price. People don't mind dropping some dollars to buy cables and wires for their expensive electronic appliances such as TV and computer.

#Strategy 7 – Consider the Size and Weight of the product

Many customers sometimes don't want to shop big items online because of the shipping fee that might be attached to it. It is often better to go for products that are light in weight and small in size. Small products are easy to package and ship. Customers want to buy more and spend less on shipping; however, if the item I too big, they have to spend a high amount on shipping, and this may deter them from buying. These are some of the details you also need to pay attention to as you prepare to stock your online store.

ECOMMERCE AND DROPSHIPPING

The decision on which products to buy can be overwhelming at times. Also, the stakes are very high. However, if you follow these strategies, you will be able to make the right decisions on the best product you should stock up. Usually, it is best to go for accessories. Many people don't know the benefits of selling accessories such as HDMI cables, Hubs, and USB cords, etc. the items are quite inexpensive. So, it is possible to increase their prices and make a high margin profit from selling them. Many people often stay away from bigger items that involve hundreds of dollars, but they do not have any issue buying the items accessories.

CHAPTER SEVEN

STEP 4: CREATE YOUR BUSINESS AND BRAND

A business is created by following due processes. To build an e-commerce business, you also need to engage in certain activities regardless of whether it is virtual or not. in this chapter, I will be taking you through two important parts of e-commerce, which is your online store creation and the process of creating a formidable brand for your business. If you want to run a successful business, then you cannot do without a good brand. Your brand will connect you and your customers together. Having set up your business, and it is ready for work, the next is to start creating a mental picture in the minds of your prospective buyers. So, the business creation is just the physical establishment of the store, while branding should be considered as the creation of the driving force that will appeal to your customers and bring them to buy from you.

SETTING UP YOUR ONLINE BUSINESS

Before you start selling online, there are specific steps you need to go through to make your business ready. Follow thoroughly to know the necessary steps to take.

- **Business Registration**

The first step is to choose a name for your business and register the company. You need to register your company so that you can have access to some benefits on tax and legal protections. Hence, you should make sure you do it.

- **Create a Name for Your Store**

You have the opportunity to use a different name for your online store that is different from your company's name. however, it is quite better to use the same name for both your company and your store. Moreover, whatever name you plan to use should work in line with your niche, and don't rush the process of choosing your brand name, but rather select your brand name carefully.

- **Obtain Your Business Licenses**

There are licenses that you need to get for you to operate your business. If you don't know how to go about it, you can approach the Small Business Association. There are lots of resources with them which will help you on how to go about the license processing. The association also has a mentor program to help new business persons, and also, they offer some courses on the basis of the business. You should endeavor to get people ahead of you that will mentor you. Their advice will help you because they have a lot of experience about how it works. Hence they will be helpful to you on how best you go about it.

- **Obtain your Employer Identification Number**

For your business to be able to open a bank account and file business taxes in April, you need to get your Employer Identification Number. The EIN is compulsory regardless of whether you will be employing or not for your business. The EIN serves similarly to your business social security number. The EIN is always unique, and it is useful whenever you want to file any important paperwork.

- **Get the Most Suitable Vendor**

Identify the best vendors you would want to work with for long. Remember, there will be lots of competitions for you to handle online, and one way to deal with it is to have quality products at cost-effective prices. You should get vendors that will supply quality products that you need or the materials that you need to produce the products, and at the same time, the vendors should not be too expensive for you to manage cost and earn a profit. If you are yet to get the best vendor you need, you may shop around until you see one.

- **Create Your Business Logo**

You need to create a logo for your business. It is not in your capacity to create the logo personally. You should hire a professional designer to help come up with a thoughtful logo that will represent the ideal of your business. You need to be sure that your logo is not the same as any other business' logo.

Above are basically the processes you need to take to create your business. Now, when your business is ready, you need to brand it and make it unique among thousands of businesses. The type of brand you create for your business will determine how well it would be during the course of you running the business.

CREATING A FORMIDABLE BRAND

A formidable brand is simply a trusted brand. Why do you think lots of Americans and others still patronize the age-long McDonalds? With all the new fast food businesses around us, most people still maintain their loyalty to the old restaurant. It is a simple concept you can also understand. They have just created a trusted brand and impression on their customers, and that is why many of their customers will pass through many hamburgers outlets until they see a McDonald's outlet and walk in to pick their hamburger. You are not selling hamburgers online, most probably. However, the same rule works for you as well. If you are able to bring your customers to your site for the first time, you should be able to make them come back without you necessarily bring them yourself. That is the working of Brand!

Why You Need Branding

There are lots of e-commerce businesses, and you are all selling the same or similar products. The question now is, how do you stand out among this competition? Although we have Amazon, JVZoo, eBay, ClickBank, and many more, all in the same online business, they, however, show different results. Why some of these companies are making millions of dollars, some are not even making anything close to it. The truth is that successful brands have very strong branding. People believe in whatever product they recommend, with the mindset that they will get the quality of their money. One way these successful companies are doing promoting their brands is through the endorsement of celebrities. Hence, how do you have a strong brand that can always stand out regardless of the competition? Below are the steps that will guide you.

- **Set out your core values and determine your specific audience**

You should have plans to make e-commerce business a stay for yourself. If you want it to be the means of making, then you have got to set up values that can stand the test of time. The first question to ask yourself is. "What do you want your business to be known for?" Are you interested in solving problems? Or do you just want to sell products online and make your bucks? Who and who are you targeting to be your customers? Do you want to create an online store for the wealthy or those who earn less? The best way to build your business is to have the right set of people you want to sell to in mind. Your values should contain things you will never compromise on. You should set up your values on what will always make your first-time customers come back to you, and this can only happen if you are solving their problems and not adding to them. Whatever values you set, you should make sure you follow it because once your customers notice that there is a turn in your business approach, they will also turn on you.

- **Set up a valuable Domain Name and give your website an awesome outlook**

It is best for you to get yourself a branded domain. Make sure your domain name is valuable to your business. A valuable domain name will be a name that anyone first-timer can always remember. The name should also stand for the values of your business, and it should stand-in for your brand in any situation. To generate ideas for your domain name, you can employ the help of Shopify's free business name generator. Also, your website should have a well-planned and creatively staged up design that will make it look elegant and alluring. You should not attempt to make use of the WordPress theme, which will not give you a great outlook and also place your business at a security risk. Many people make the mistake of overlooking these elements during their set up. Your domain name and your website outlook are important for the success of your brand image.

- **Create a Unique Logo**

As I have mentioned earlier, your logo must be unique. It is what will anchor your brand. The logo you create will be the identity of your business online. The features of a good logo include strength, iconicity, and representative of a brand.

- **Create a "Why" statement**

Having set up your website, you need to start with the *Why* of your business. In the real sense, people will not buy what you sell, but they will buy the reason behind what you sell. Hence, why it is quite important in the process of making your sales. When your customers understand the *Why* of your products, and they believe in it for its authenticity, they will grow in their loyalty toward you and bring more for you to do. Your brand needs to gather your customer's loyalty if it is to stand the test of time.

- **Create powerful content**

One other way to maintain your brand and give it its best look is always to create great content. Make your writings on your website memorable. Make your audience react to your writings by hitting them deep and attracting their attention. Your content on your website should work in alignment with the values of your business, let the content present the uniqueness of your products, and make them take action through your content.

- **Create your Website policy**

Everything on your website should maintain consistency. You need to create policies for your website so that it can maintain a specific outlook that will make it unique. The intention is to create consistency on your website. Your consistency should reflect in the style of "call-to-action" you want to adopt, how the call-to-action button will be used to convert customers should also have the same pattern. Your method of paragraphing and headings should all conform to a particular format. All these will give your customers a great experience.

CHAPTER EIGHT

STEP 5: CREATING YOUR ONLINE STORE

The fifth step to take after registering your business and planning your brand is to build your store. Building your store include you registering the domain name you pick, and any other redirect URLs that are essential. Building your online store requires you to use an e-Commerce software, and your choice of design needs to be compatible with the e-commerce software you want to use. Your online store will serve the same function as a physical store. The only difference is that it is virtual, and it is always opened to any customer who wishes to shop. There are steps you need to take to have an impressive online store. I will take you through the steps so that you will not end up creating a dummy online store.

Step 1 – Get the Best E-commerce Website Builder

There are many e-commerce website builders. The website builders are online software that will give enable you to create a personal online store without any need for skills on coding or other knowledge on advanced tech on computers. With your business idea and a fast and reliable internet connection, you are good to go work an e-commerce website builder. Due to the increase in the number of e-commerce builders, you need to identify the one that is most suitable for your online store. There are disparities among the builders in regard to their prices, and reliability. The popular ones among them include Shopify, Wix, BigCommerce, Squarespace, Weebly, etc. I will discuss these builders in a later chapter.

Step 2 – Choose the Most Suitable Plan for Your Business
After selecting a builder for the creation of your online store, you will be required to choose a plan that will enable you to build your website. There are different levels of plan you will see, and these levels have their specific features. Usually, the more expensive a plan is, the more features it stands to have. The kind of plan you choose should be based on the size of your business and the future plans you have in

your business. For your online e-commerce store, you will be going for a paid plan. The reason for this is because your website requires you to upload and sell products; this is more complicated than an ordinary website. Plans start on a monthly basis, and the builders offer a different amount. Wix eCommerce charge from $20 per month, while Shopify and BigCommerce charge$30 monthly. However, the kinds of features you need should determine the plan you go for.

Step 3 – Select Your Domain Name

You need your name to help your customers identify your store online. Your domain name must be good enough to attract you to the customers you need. The domain name you choose is what your customers will see in the address bar and when they search for you on Google. When you choose your domain name, you should follow the following steps:

- *Use the right country code. It is advisable you use .com if your target is global customers, you only need to use a specific country code if you are planning to sell to in that country only.*
- *Don't include a brand or product's name in your domain name. It may lead to a legal issue.*
- *Choose a special name that will make you stand out. However, don't pick a name that will make you go*

> obscure when people need to search for products that you sell.
> - *You should include a keyword in your domain name. This will earn you a place in Google ranking. The more people see you, the more traffic you will get, and the more people you have on your website, the more sale you tend to make.*

Note that you need to set a date for you to remember when your domain name will expire (it expires yearly), and you should renew the registration before it expires.

Step 4 – Choose and Customize your E-commerce template

You need to pick a suitable template, which is also called a theme for your store. The builders all have their specific themes that will give your site a great look. While you select the template for your site, provide answers to these questions:

What features do I want to see in my store?

What form of homepage do I want?

How do I want my customers to navigate in my store?

The features are what is important to your store. They include maps, a page that will tell about the business (About Us page), videos, etc.

The homepage is the first part of your store that your customers will contact. Do you want it to be a video or a slideshow or image? You should choose.

The navigation method is important. You need to make your customers see the products they need as soon as possible. Make sure every product is arranged in a way that your customers can easily access them. Have a good page layout with the direction of a well-arranged product.

Also, having selected your template, you need to set up personal customization of your theme. There are tools for customization on the website. When you customize, you are simply altering the font, text size, images, color scheme, features, product positioning, and many more.

Step 5 – Place Your Products

The next thing to do is to add your products to the website. The online store builder gives you total control over your product's page. When you place your products online, you are basically adding Four/five things:

The product's Name

The Price

The Category

The Weight of the product

File (this is optional. It is for products that can be downloaded, such as eBook).

These disparities in the number of products you can upload using a specific online store builder. The online builders also have limitations on the number of options you have for a product (which is a similar product with different size or color), and for the number of products invariance. Before you select your e-commerce store builder, you should check the one that will suit your business option in this regard.

As you upload your products, there are three key elements you need to pay attention to. These are:

The description of the product: Make sure that the description gets a hold on the buyers. Stay away from clichés, long sentences, and any form of complex vocabularies. Your description must be concise but detailed. It is a strong selling point of products online. Remember, you will not be there to convince a buyer to buy like you would have done in a physical shop. You also need to make sure that your description works with SEO to easily draw traffic to you.

Your product Image: the image you are planning to upload should adequately portray the product. You should make use of a high-quality picture, let there be a 360-degree option so that your buyers can easily see the products from all angles. There should be a zooming option for buyers to look into the product.

The Category of the Products: you should categorize your products in a different area. It will fit in. The categorization will help customers to access a product easily. At the same time, you should be careful about having so many categorizations so that you won't confuse your customers.

Step 6 – Create a payment method

Having set up your products, you need to set the means of payment. There will be no cashier to receive the payment from your customers. With the help of the online store builders, you can do this easily. There are many payment options, and the builder will connect you with them. Thee payment options we have included, PayPal, MasterCard,

Visa, and Apple Pay. To receive payment from your buyers, there are three popular methods:

- *The Merchant Account and Payment gateway:* with this, you will partner with a bank, and the bank will receive the payment on your behalf while they will channel it to your business account.
- *Payment gateway packages:* this involves you using all-in-one software. Your store's shopping cart will be connected to the card processing network.
- *Credit card payment processing:* you can work with a service that is integrated with your store's check out. If your builder is Shopify, you can use the Shopify payment gateway. This method does not require your buyers to leave your website to pay.

Step 7 – Set Your Shipping Settings

This is the part that deals with the delivering of the products your buyers have paid for. There are different shipping options depending on the online store builder you use. Shipping a product requires you to add an origin address and the type of the package. There are different shipping options you can select. There are the following:

Free Shipping: This is not compulsory. You should only go for it if you can afford it. It is also a way of getting more customers. If you are offering free shipping, you should set a particular amount of order a person can place. You should never ship freely at the expense of your business.

Flat Rate: This option involves charging the same rate for all products .it is also good for marketing. You may state that the shipping fee is $10 for some specific states or continents regardless of the good and its quantity. It will work well for you if your store is filled with similar products.

Real-time Quotes: This involves shipping prices based on some factors such as the weight, sizes, or destination of the products. This is the option many customers prefer for their transparency. If your store is filled with products of varying sizes, it is the best option.

There are different levels of shipping you can offer your buyers. If the customer wants to get his or her products faster, he or she may have to pay more. There are many courier services that can help you with the shipping. Some of them are Canada Post, FedEx, and USPS.

CHAPTER NINE

STEP 6: BRINGING CUSTOMERS TO YOUR STORE

Every store dispenses its products to customers. If there are no customers, the products are going nowhere, and to sell you're your products, you need to attract customers to yourself. A key to bringing customers to your online store is through e-commerce marketing. E-marketing is done with the help of SEO and the visibility you have gained online. Successful online stores often invest in online marketing. Digital marketing is the key for you to keep seeing a flow of buyers approaching your store. There are many steps you can take with e-commerce marketing to boost your sales. The best form of marketing you need must protect your online reputation and brand. One key element you need is to be easily accessed online by prospective buyers. When people are simply exploring social media, they should be able to locate you without stress. The more people see you, the more you will remain on their minds. To attract customers to yourself, you should follow the following tips.

Be Easily Accessible Online and Improve Your Online Presence: Make people find you easily. The first impression always lasts longer on people's minds. When they have access to you in a search engine, and they learn the good things about you, and how you can help solve their problems, they will think of doing business with you. You should make yourself rank in Google ranking and search engines.

Also, look at how present you are online presently and make needed adjustments. You need to make sure that web searches show you in its results whenever people search for your business or any other business that is related to yours. Your target is to show up dominantly in any body's search result. One other way to increase your presence is by interacting with an online audience. This will help you build a strong relationship with them. You should be participating online consistently to boost your presence.

Have an Attractive Introduction Online: Wherever you are present online, you should write concise but detailed information about your business. Make the people online want to learn more about your business. Your introduction should be filled with keywords that most buyers may want to search for online. Your introduction should include what your business does and the target audience. Let the readers know the distinctive features of your business and why they have to trust it. From your introduction, there should be an assurance that you can deliver. You should also add information such as your business or domain name that will make it easier for prospective buyers to locate you.

Always Create Content: One other way to make your people know you are to create content that will lead people to your website. You can invest in content that will be posted on blogs, probably weekly, on Twitter, or Facebook. The contents should contain a shareable link that will direct the readers to your website where they can easily see the product they want.

Be Available to Monitor Your Online Reputation: You need to take note of how well your business name is growing among people. Always look for what people are saying about your business, and be ready to accept criticism with the mindset of improving your business around the criticism. Through social media, you can now monitor the mention of your business name online. You just need to make sure that your business keeps a good image before everyone to have a lasting impression on them. There are online-mention alerts that will help you know when your name is mentioned online. you can utilize Google Alerts, Social Mention, or Bing Alerts

Create an Excellent Customer Care Platform: One way to attract customers is to care for them. When they come, your ability to make the first set of customers' stay will help you. When your customers are satisfied, they will find it easy and propelling to bring more customers. Have a customer care platform that will always be available to attend to the need of your customers, their questions, and feedback. Whenever a customer has a complaint, you should be ready to attend to the issue and make the customer leave happier than he or she came.

Set Up Promos: Many people love discounts and promos. The result of promos is usually a soar in the number of customers of a business. This result is not based on the reduction in the amount paid. But it is a result of the psychological effect of promo on the buyer. When people hear the word "free," there is a way they naturally become excited that they end up connecting with something and may even start a relationship with the thing. Your promos may come in the form of free shipping, or probably you give discount coupons. You may make these promos available to new clients, and this is to make them make their first purchase with which you must win them over by the quality of your service. This means that the promo or discount should not affect the quality of your service and products.

Make Use of E-mails: Email marketing is one of the most effective means of attracting customers to your business.

ECOMMERCE AND DROPSHIPPING

People often remember the company's emails sent to them. You should send emails about new products, about your promos and sales, you may also recommend products that are similar to what your customers bought through an email. Through emails, you will make them know that they have had a deal somewhere that they need to go back to.

CHAPTER TEN

STEP 7: CARRYING OUT MARKETING STRATEGIES FOR YOUR PRODUCTS ONLINE

This is the final step in the process of building your e-commerce business. You don't just promote your website. You are not trying to be an influencer. Your primary goal is to make sales, that is, to sell the products and services you offer. Hence, you need to market your products and services as well for prospective buyers to know what you have in stock. To sell your products, you need to maintain great marketing. If your product I not well promoted, it may end up remaining in your store. However, with a well-formulated promotion, your products and services will sell beyond your imagination. I have tips for you on how you can promote your products.

There are lots of methods for you to employ to promote your products and services. These ways work depending on the type of products and services you have to offer. Below are some methods you can make use of:

Utilize Google My Business

Each time your new products arrive, you can post them on your Google My Business profile. There are two methods for you to promote your products and services on Google My Business. You can post them and select the "Promotion" option, or you may just post the image of the new product or service you render on your profile. It is also possible for you to add some frequently asked questions about the product or service on your profile. The purpose is to get people to see it and come up with your website to pick whichever product they want.

Introduce a Preview of Your New products

Your loyal customers are the first go-to set of people you need to approach for your new products. They already have a taste of your products and services, making an effort to convince them for a new set will not be too challenging. You should offer your customers the opportunity to preview your new products. You may go for a pre-launch party or an online preview. You may also invite them to test the product or whatever newest service you have. This will make them feel so important that they will want to come back.

Organize Social Media Contests

Social media contests have proven to be a reliable method of attracting buyers for a new product. Social media contest will connect different buyers, and also attract the attention of new buyers who will be knowing about your business for the first time. You may organize the contests on Facebook or Instagram. The contest might come in the form of a giveaway that will make the winner the first person to use the product.

Email Marketing is Another Way

A report stated that 82% of customers are often drawn to emails from businesses. According to another report, 44% of those who received emails from a business made at least a single purchase in 2018. Using email marketing though newsletter is a great way of attracting customers to your new products and services. With an email newsletter, you will be able to share information and image of your new products.

Carry out Facebook Advertisement

Facebook has proven to be a great impressive platform for you to market your product. The social network boasts of 1.44 billion users every month. This is more than what you need to build your business. This large presence gives Facebook its stance as an important platform to promote your products and services. Facebook offers you the possibility to focus on your audience without stress. The demographic studies you might have done about the buyers you want will be easily accessed on Facebook due to the well-documented details of every user.

Give out an Upgrade or Trade-In

This will work well for a service-based business. If you operate, let's say a salon, you can give out an upgrade for your customers to test your new service without charging them. Your interest is to make them see the difference between this new service and the one they are used to.

You can make use of trade-in promotions for your product that is an upgrade of an existing one. This promotion involves incentivizing your customers to purchase your new products by using a token they possess. If the trade-in product is old, you may resell it if it is in good condition, or make use of them in the future as giveaways.

Let Your Customer's Review Circulate

Sharing your customer's reviews about your products will go a long way to help you promote the product more. When you make use of the earlier mentioned ideas, and you have the first set buyers or users of the product, tell them to review it and make sure that new prospective buyers see the reviews. You make it circulate by sharing it online. If there are testimonies from others about the products, many people will be willing to buy them.

CHAPTER ELEVEN

E-COMMERCE TOOLS FOR STARTUPS

E-commerce business requires the use of certain tools to make it perform excellently. There are numerous types of these tools that one can utilize to set up his or her online store. E-commerce business is more than you have a store, and products to sell. You also need to be able to draw the attention of your prospective buyers via the outlook and functionality of your store. In this chapter, I will be taking you through certain website builders that you can rely on to help you build the best website you need to make your fortune in the e-commerce business. There are lots of these builders you can make use of. However, I have identified five outstanding software builders you can rely on and give your online store the best outlook.

BigCommerce

BigCommerce provides easy access to the creation of an online store. It is a flexible online store builder that can accept any business regardless of its size. The software tool was created in 2009, and it has since then gained influence among many online shopping businesses. Top businesses that make use of it include Hush Puppies, Toyota, Fujitsu, etc. The tool gives new users the opportunity to use them freely for 15 days. Within this free trial days, you are allowed to place any product on displace, and you will also have access to similar features that paying users to have. BigCommerce is very easy to use. You can easily set up your store with the builder without any hassle. It is a cloud-based hosted platform, which makes it needless to download or install anything by yourself. You are only required to sign up for the service and start using the account you create.

The builder gives the easiness of accessing its features. You can easily access your dashboard and the settings that will make it easy for you to do any customization or changes you want to see. The process of adding your products, creating an avenue for orders, and designs are quite easy to access. The platform permits you to manage your products and orders. Also, you can easily handle your shipping charges, use multiple payment methods, and provide support to your customers. There is also a support channel for the users of the platform to communicate with the developers of BigCommerce. You can either have a live chat, phone call, or send them emails on whatever help you need.

One advantage of BigCommerce is that it gives you the opportunity for you as a starter to integrate with successful and established online stores such as Amazon, eBay, etc. and you do not have to pay any extra charges for any extra order made. However, the builder is primarily set on features and users' experience; as a result, its platform has a limited design. You only have access to free 7 themes to choose from. If you do not like them, you will be requested to pay.

Shopify

This is one of the biggest online store builders that are making a wave in the industry. The website developing software has a story of a small beginning, which later metamorphosed into a large business with over 4000 employees. With over 800,000 users globally, one cannot say of the obvious success rate it has. It is user-friendly, and it has popular brands as its users, among which are, Tesla, The Economist, Budweiser, etc. just like BigCommerce, Shopify also gives a free trial. However, it gives a 14-day trial rather than the 15 days' trial of BigCommerce. For these 14 days, you will not be required to pay for their services while you set up your store and place your products for sale. After the 14 days, you are to decide whether the service meets up with your expectations or not.

Shopify is easy to use. It is designed with a guiding interface, which will put you through on how to build your online store. It gives a comprehensive explanation of whatever needs to be done during the process of registration and setup. It has well-designed features that make it perfect for use. Shopify stands out for its introduction of the Point of Sale (POS). This feature permits business owners to make sales and also receive payment from different locations and vendors with security. This feature is available in all paid plans, and it makes it easy for you to present your business and products to many people. You can also seek support from its team through various means, such as telephone, emails, live chat, social media such as Twitter.

It has an advantage in its design features. It offers ten free themes; with 60 other themes you need to pay for. You may, however, get more themes online. It has a high versatility rate among the many e-commerce builders. It gives benefits that include dropshipping setup, Point of Sale, and free SSL. However, compared to other website builders, Shopify has a higher credit card fee, and it requires an added transaction fee if you fail to use the internal payment system. Also, you may have difficulty as a starter with advanced store customization.

WiX

The Wix platform was launched in 2006, and it has a fully hosted site-building service. With this, you do not need any hosting provider to run your shop. It has a space among restaurants and healthcare service providers. It has over 10,000 users. It gives 14 days' trial for new users to build your e-commerce website. Its service is free. You can build

ECOMMERCE AND DROPSHIPPING

your website without any payment; however, for you to engage in an online business store, you need to upgrade to its premium plan to be able to use its full features.

It is easy to use, and you can easily carry out your customization with little or no knowledge of designs. You can easily edit your shop and even create it from either your phone or PC. Its features include inventory tracking, awesome looking storefront, global shipping taxes, multiple payment methods, and coupons, and discounts. The builder offers different services, including hosting, plugins, hosting, updates, etc. It does not have any live chat support.

Wix is beneficial for its ease of use. It is self-explanatory for you as a first-timer. There are tips and additional information that will guide you in the process of creating your website and setting up your store. It gives access to over 500 templates (both free and premium). More importantly, it offers a cost-effective service. It offers e-commerce plans from as low as $20 per month, and it gives up to 20GB storage. Its bandwidth is unlimited, and it offers a one-year free domain. With all of these, you can easily build your online store at a minimal cost. The disadvantage lies in n the fact that it is too rudimentary. Going for advanced customization, which will give your website a better look, is quite difficult. Also, it is not primarily designed for e-commerce; hence, many big businesses do not find it suitable. It is great for any starter, and small businesses, however, it does not work well for a large business.

Weebly

It was introduced in 2007, and presently, it gives strength to millions of web pages. Just like WiX, the services rendered by Weebly does not stop at the level of e-commerce store creation, but also to all kinds of websites. It does not give free days' trial. However, it offers a 30-day return policy. If you do not enjoy its service, after 30 days of use, you will be refunded. It is not technical to operate. The process of customization and another process of building your store are quite easy and accessible. It is flexible, however, quite difficult to get, unlike WiX. Weebly does not work generally like WiX; it has restrictions.

The service offers features such as product configurator, management of order and clients, and SEO options, campaigns and promotions management, and multi-store support with a lot more. It gives access to support. You can easily chat, send an email, and get assistance through phone calls. Weebly is affordable. It offers as little as $12 per month for its online e-commerce store. It offers free domain and $100 credits in Google Ads. It is created with a lot of templates. It, however, does not provide the best service for advanced modifications, and for large businesses that require deeper features. Startups have no problem using it because it is specifically for them.

Squarespace

The service was created in 2003, and it has experienced consistent growth. It offers a 14-day trial for you to access most of its features. With Squarespace, anyone can easily create an e-commerce website. However, you can't publish them, and you cannot make the search engine robot carry out indexing of the pages. It contains a steep learning curve, and it is not fully users friendly. However, if you have little

ECOMMERCE AND DROPSHIPPING

experience with e-commerce store management, you will not have any issue with it.

Squarespace gives lots of features when you are on its premium account. The premium plan gives you a free domain, unlimited product support, and SSL. However, it does not meet up with the standard of top website builders. It has lots of benefits that include, free transaction, Orders API, integrated accounting, products on Instagram, etc. it has a 24/7 standby support. It does not have phone assistance, but emails are welcome, while live chat works once a while.

Squarespace has a well-detailed analytics section. If your website is not for retail stores, you will enjoy this. It also offers great designs, with the consistent release of beautiful and elegant themes. You can carry out modifications on the templates, although you cannot customize them fully. However, it does not meet up in terms of navigation, features, and third-party app integration. It only supports PayPal and Apple Pay as payment methods. These are limitations to an online store.

ECOMMERCE AND DROPSHIPPING

Among the popular website builders, Shopify and WiX are quite great for startups and SMEs. If you are considering your expenses, you may select WiX or Weebly. However, they do not offer the best features that BigCommerce has. Note that aside from these tools, there are other tools you can rely on for your hosting.

CHAPTER TWELVE

CHALLENGES FACING E-COMMERCE

Many successful businesses are products of challenges. To build your business, there are certain hurdles you need to overcome. Climbing these ladders is what you need to stand out in your process of building your business. Similarly, e-commerce business has lots of obstacles and challenges you need to overcome if you want to make it big. In this chapter, I have identified some common challenges that many startups face in the process of building their business. I have also given my specific solutions to deal with each challenge. Whenever your business faces any of these challenges, you need to be calm and understand that it is surmountable.

Challenge 1 – Verification of Identity Online

The first challenge you are likely to face is how to identify a visitor and his or her interest. You want to know if the person comes in with his or her real details. It is possible that the visitor comes in with a fake identity. You will need to have an online identity verification to know every visitor.

The Solution

You need to take specific steps to ascertain the information of the customer. To get the information, there is software designed to give you the best solutions to the issue. LexisNexis helps to deal with any fraudulent attempts online. It verifies the details about the identity of a person. It has electronic identity verification, instant authentication, identity check, and SSN verification. You can easily deal with any possible hacker with this tool.

Challenge 2 – Analysis of Competitors

You will be facing a lot of competitors in the e-commerce business. Most of you will most likely be involved in similar products and services. Hence, the need for you to be different. This is always an area of challenge for most startups. Competitor analysis is what helps to keep up with the competition. You need to find out how best you can stand out from the competition.

The Solution

Your competition analysis should involve the kinds of products your competitors are selling, the price they sell the products, the platforms they are using to make their sales to their customers, their methods of generating leads, and are they engaging in any promotions for their businesses? You should find out the products that are being demanded highly, and remove those that are not in demand. Also, go the extra mile to give an exceptional deal to your customers to be unique.

Challenge 3 – Building Customer Loyalty

Customers are the life wire of any business. It is often better to maintain your customer base than to start looking around for new customers. It will cost you more than 3 times an effort to get a new customer than you retaining your old customers. Also, the chance of selling to your existing customer is quite high, while you have less than 20% chance of getting to sell to a new customer. Hence, you need to have a customer base that is loyal to your business and products. The question now is: What means can you use to build trust with your buyers?

The Solution

The key to having the loyalty of your customers is to give them the best customer service they can ever get. Make every first sale a memorable one. Make them want to come for more. They should be happy that they are patronizing you. When they see the worth of their money, they will trust you with their future choices. Also, you should do the following to earn their trust.

- Make your customers have access to you. Your address, contact details, should be available for your customers to see on your website.
- Always stay online for your customers to see you. You should blog regularly. People will be able to relate with you through it and see you from another perspective than being a seller only.
- Create emails to build a connective relationship with your customers. Connect with them by sending them personalized emails.

Challenge 4 – Dealing with Product Return and Refund

ECOMMERCE AND DROPSHIPPING

A report by ComScore says that over 60% of online buyers claimed they are interested in the return policy of an online store before they buy from the store. Also, some buyers leave some stores because of their delivery dates. Also, ComScore reported that most buyers don't want to wait for more than 5 days to receive their package. Many customers make a return, and most of these customers are not first-timers but those who are already buying from the store. The essence of this is to show how important product return and refund policy are to customers. There are many large and growing businesses that are notable for their return policies. Examples are Costco, Nordstrom, and REI.

The Solution

Avoid tricking your customers about your return policy. Let them have access to the detail policies guiding the process of returning items. You may add FAQs to make them accessible to any possible questions that may bother them. Don't be vague in your instructions, so that they will not be any misleading. Your policies should be explicit for your customers to understand. Don't let your customers feel like they have something more to know. Give them all they may need.

Challenge 5 – Prices and Shipping

The prices of products and the shipping cost are one area of challenge for many startups. Many giant businesses like Amazon, eBay, can afford to sell a product with the same amount as your business and still give out free shipping for the same product since they have what it takes to do that. They have set up shipping warehouses globally, and they just pick up orders from the nearest facility to the buyer. As a small business, this is a great challenge that you need to stand up against, and how do you cope with it?

The Solution

Become creative in your approach. You should identify local courier businesses that will help you deliver your products faster to your customers at a very competitive rate. When you use the Roadie App, you will be able to deliver competitively more than the popular couriers. It helps to provide an innovative means of delivery at a cost-effective rate.

Challenge 6 – Issues with Retailers and Manufacturers

One major challenge many online stores face is the activities of the retailers and manufacturers. Most of the businesses get their products from the retailers and manufacturers, and often, these retailers and manufacturers sell the same products to the consumers directly. This affects the sales of the online store.

The Solution

You should have an agreement in your contract with the manufacturers and retailers that will prevent them from selling to the consumers. You can also opt for the retailers and manufacturers that will most likely not sell to the consumers directly.

Challenge 7 – The Security of Your Data

A data breach is one of the most challenges many online stores face. It is often difficult to overcome technical issues. You need to be wary of attackers to prevent your site from viruses and exposing important information. This will impact your business negatively if it is not attended to rightly and appropriately.

The Solution

The first step to take is always to back up your data. Security plugins help to prevent websites from being hacked. You should install them. There are many options for security plugins you can have, such as BulletProof Security, Wordfence, etc.

The internet space is filled with a lot of challenges that one must overcome to emerge victoriously. You only need to follow certain steps to make it work out fine for you. Do not panic whenever you encounter any challenge. All you need to do is take the right approach to deal with it, and you would have successfully saved yourself from a deadly situation.

CHAPTER THIRTEEN

AVOIDING E-COMMERCE MISTAKES

As a startup, you are likely to make mistakes. These mistakes may have grave consequences on your business, and to avoid the possible ripple effects that the mistakes you can make will lead to, you need to deal with them from scratch, so they never keep up their ugly faces. Usually, there are two forms of mistakes many people make in e-commerce business – management and conversion mistakes. There is a difference between conversion and traffic. The traffic on your website is the number of people that come to your website, while conversion happens when they stay to buy. Many people get people to their website, but they often fail to have them stay and buy from them. In order for you to avoid this, you need to watch out for the possible mistakes you are likely to make. Below are some of the mistakes you are likely to make.

Wasting time on Needless Activities

This is a common mistake among many e-commerce businesses. Many e-commerce store owners realized this mistake during one of "Growth Hacking Academy." They have been wasting time on activities that are not necessary during the period of building their online store. Some of them spend time on designing their logo, which is not important as much as their content. There are specific activities you need to give time to like, making your business known by others and creating engaging content that will make them stay. Always ask yourself this question while you are building your online store: What relevance does this activity have on my business? The response will let you know how much time you are supposed to spend while you are on it.

Being in Charge of all Activities

ECOMMERCE AND DROPSHIPPING

Obviously, you would want the activities on your website to go according to your way. It is great. You want to get the respect of others, that is also fine. However, that should be a later thought. For you to grow your business, you need to think about a lot of things. The list of your thoughts should contain the following: Concepts, Strategy, SEO/PPC campaigns, Community management, analytics, Website administration, social media, maintenance of your website, email marketing for your products and website, etc.

Looking at this list, I believe you understand that you cannot do everything yourself. Each of them is a profession on its own that requires a professional. Hence, you are expected to get people who are vast in the fields to operate them. Many e-commerce owners think of money, and they try to fill these positions alone. You trying to do this would mean you must learn everything, and as a result, you are busy wasting time, which is not infinite. You need to understand the value of time and face the specific area you will perform well while you get the skill of others to excel at those areas you can't handle. When you distribute the works, and you focus on the one, you have strength in most, you would be more productive, and your business will grow. If you can't afford to employ the professionals, you may utilize the service of freelancers. That would save you a lot of money while you experience a soar in your business.

Not Sending Enough Mails

The mistake many business owners make is the thought that they will be blocked for sending emails consistently to their customers. No, they won't block you. You need to apply strategy to the process of sending the emails. There is a rule by Vilfredo Pareto called the Pareto Principle. The rule is an 80/20 formula that states that for every activity, almost 80% of the results come from 20% of the causes. This means that, for the 80% sales you make in your business, 20% of your customers are to be considered responsible for them. You should adopt this principle in your bid to send emails.

You should adopt a segmentation principle, where you will segment your customers into two parts and identify those that are loyal and consistent and those that are not. You should send more emails to the 20% of customers that buy more than the other 80%. Your customers that are loyal will never block you for sending them more emails. And they will be connected more with you that they will keep buying from your store.

Not Creating Strong Product's Descriptions

Online store differs from physical stores in the sense that the buyers will not meet you, the store owner to discuss a product. In a physical store, you could easily convince a prospective buyer through the words of your mouth. However, in an online store, what you write about a product is what matters. You need to be able to convince your customers about a product based on how you describe the product. Your choice of words and images should work toward achieving that. Your description should be concise yet detailed. And the image should be alluring and detailed that the buyer will not be left with any question unanswered.

Your product should not be targeted at telling the buyer about the product primarily. It should be selling the product to them. Let the buyers know the reasons they need to buy the product. Also, your choice of image should be clear and should be attractive. Make sure the image you set up shows the exact outlook of the product the buyer is seeking. Avoid using images with low quality. The picture should have a great *Composition*, which will make it easy to zoom in on the product, and they should be a *Background* that will contrast with the product. The background of the product should be different from the product. Let your picture have a great *Focus*; that is, it should be sharp enough. The right format for most web pages are JPG and GIF, make use of any of these so that your customers will not have any issues with them. And you should *Compress* the image so that it will give room for fast loading. You need to make the details of your products available and accessible to all buyers; this way, they will gain access to what they want to buy and know whether it is actually what they need or not.

Not Tracing Your Customers Movement on Your Website

The last mistake I will mention is not knowing the activities of your customers on your website. Before now, many online store owners were not aware of the movements of their customers on their sites. However, the introduction of Hotjar, Luckyorange, Mouseflow, among others, created a new phase in digital marketing. With these tools, you can easily know the movement and activities of your website visitors and customers. Hotjar is the most popular among the tools. Hotjar has a tool called Heatmaps, which shows the part of an online store that visitors interact with most. Also, it will reveal the device that your visitors are connecting from. If you record this, you will have a better insight into how your customers are navigating through your store, and this will help for a future reference. There is a feature that works with forms, and for every form you have, you will know when your visitors don't fill them in anymore.

The results you get from these features will let you know the reasons why your customers are not buying. If your delivery forms are not being filled in, you can check whether it is because it is too long that they had to drop it. You can know whether there is a problem with the loading speed of a particular page, and that is discouraging your visitors to go ahead with it. Hence, they leave the page and visit other pages. All these will give you the answers you need to work on for your business growth.

You must be well-informed as an online store owner to stay ahead in your business. Stay away from these avoidable mistakes and see your e-commerce business soaring higher than you could have ever thought of. The secret to increasing in business is to understand how the business works — nothing more, nothing less.

PART TWO

AMASSING WEALTH WITH THE DROPSHIPPING MODEL

CHAPTER FOURTEEN

GETTING TO KNOW DROPSHIPPING

Dropshipping is an e-commerce business model that enables a company to run without having a store. In dropshipping, a company sells online, yet it does not maintain any inventory, have as a warehouse to keep its products, and it is not in charge of shipping the product bought to the consumers. The dropshipping model enables a store to make sales by purchasing the item that customers ordered online from a third party, and they make sure that the third party delivers the item to the customers. The seller does not get involved in the selling of the product directly. The seller who has an online store will partner with a dropship supplier (the third party) who produce specific products, to sell, and ship the products whenever it is requested.

ECOMMERCE AND DROPSHIPPING

Dropshipping is used by many small retailers online that generally sell in low quantities to their buyers. When they receive a large order for a specific product, they will have to approach the manufacturer or a wholesaler of the product to ship the goods to the customer directly. Also, the model is often used for goods that are expensive. Most sellers on auction sites also utilize the dropship model. It helps them to deliver the products they have without sending the goods to their buyers directly.

Dropshipping differs from the standard retail model in the sense that, while the standard retail model is concern with taking the orders from the buyer, packaging the products, and make sure it is shipped to the customers, the dropship model involves the online store owner gets orders from customers, but take these orders to another party, who sells the needed products and make sure that the third party delivers the items to their buyers.

Dropshipping is an attractive business model that nullifies the need for the store owner to keep a physical store or spends highly on stocks in the process of starting the business. All an online store owner needs to do is have the means to access the internet (laptop), and a strong internet connection. However, it is also possible for a store that has physical stores to utilize a dropship model. This will help them to free their resources and space they will need for other products.

WHY YOU SHOULD ENGAGE IN DROPSHIPPING

I will be taking you through the advantages of dropshipping, which doubles as the reasons I believe you need to engage in dropshipping. The business model has a lot of benefits that make it a viable option for anyone willing to invest in the e-commerce business. Dropshipping gives you as an aspiring entrepreneur, the easiness to do business. You have the opportunity to test various ideas you may have with little or no downside, and this gives you adequate experience with your method of choosing and marketing products that are often demanded. I have identified more reasons why you should make dropshipping an interest.

It Involves Easy processes

The business is quite easy to set up without any stress whatsoever. It is easier than dealing with a physical store since you are not dealing with some functions such as managing or getting a warehouse, packaging your products and shipping them, tracking your inventory for accountability, dealing with inbound shipments, and returns, among others. Dropshipping only involves 3 steps, which are:

Identify the supplier

Create your online store; and,

Sell to the buyers

It Is Less Expensive to Establish

The conventional standard retail model involves costs that are related to the process of setting up and operating the store. Part of the operations includes buying your inventory. However, dropshipping does not require this. It is a business model you can start with next to nothing. You are not expected to buy ant products to start selling online. You only need to source products and take orders from buyers. All you need to do in dropshipping is to spend on your website and its operations. Also, since you are not into buying of inventory to resell, you stand to face less risk in the dropshipping model.

It Involves Low Overhead Costs

Since there is no need for buying products to fill your warehouse, and you don't have to get a warehouse, you will have a low overhead cost to manage. Most of the successful dropshipping businesses are run from homes. This only requires the owner to get a PC and internet connection to be able to stay online and connect with prospective buyers and sell. There are fewer recurring expenses to manage the business. Although, as the business grows, the expenses will increase; however, it is never as much as a standard retail business model. Most times, you will only have to focus on the fixed expenses for managing your website, and whenever you need to add more features that will empower your business growth, you will spend a little bit more.

It Has a Low Risk

Dropshipping risk is quite low compared to the conventional retail model. If you fail to sell the products, you are not losing, and you have less pressure about the need to sell.

It Gives Room for Flexibility of Location

If you are engaged in dropshipping business, you are free from being tied down to a particular location. There is a kind of independence that you tend to enjoy. You can basically run the business from anywhere. All you need to do is make sure you have your laptop and internet connection. You have no employees, no warehouse, and no products to monitor. All that you need is to be able to communicate with your suppliers and customers.

You Can Sell Various Types of Products

In dropshipping, you are not restricted. For every product you want to sell, you will only need to get a dropship supplier for it. You cannot be restricted from selling one product because of the capital involved. You are free to sell as much as possible and mix them up. When you sell different products, remember that the suppliers for each will deal with the delivery.

You Can Scale Your Business Faster and Easily

You do not need to make more sales, to earn more profits and invest more before you can scale your business higher in dropshipping. You are not stocking products, and neither do you have any many expenses to handle. All you need to do is get more orders and send them to your dropship suppliers to deliver to your customers. The more orders you get, the more profits you make, and you have more time and resources to make your business grow easily.

There is a Reduction in The Losses Made from Damaged Goods

Dropshipping involves the goods moving from the suppliers directly to the customers. Hence, there is less risk of goods damage because the goods are not being moved. The shipment steps are very minimal.

THE LIMITING FACTORS TO DROPSHIPPING

There are certain disadvantages of dropshipping. These disadvantages may want to make you give up on the business and think of any other alternative. The knowledge of these disadvantages will aid you as you make an effort to run a successful dropshipping business.

It Offers Lower Profit Margin

Unlike the wholesaling and manufacturing model, dropshipping gives you a lower profit margin. This is because you are likely to be charged higher by the suppliers or manufacturers for dropshipping the products to the customers. This will affect your income margin, and you need to prepare for it. Also, competition from others may likely lead to low profit. Since dropshipping requires low startup capital, many businesses would prefer selling at a lower rate for them to increase their sales. You will have to spend more to stand out and also sell less as the customers would expect you to make your profit.

You Bear the Liability When Issues Arise

The customers are dealing with you online. They only know your company; they do not know the supplier. If there is an issue, the customers will blame your company, and this will affect you directly. Hence, it is often important for any online store engaging in the dropshipping model to carefully select the right supplier.

You Lack Absolute Control Over Your Brand

It is important to satisfy your customers. And most importantly, you need to present your brand rightly before your buyers. However, dropshipping does not give you the opportunity to monitor your brand adequately. The packaging and delivery of your products are not done by you. It is the suppliers that represent your business when a buyer orders for a product. The manner a supplier presents the product to the customer determines the way your business will be perceived. This is another reason you must enlist the service of a trustworthy supplier who will always make an effort to keep your brand's image everywhere.

Issues with Shipping Complexities

Selling multiple products actually helps to build a business and makes a lot of sales. However, it also has an adverse effect. If you have a lot of suppliers for your products, you will be charged varyingly by them based on certain factors such as the location, the product's type, and others. In a case where a customer orders for more than one product that you can only get from different suppliers, you will have to pay the suppliers separately. If you make an effort to transfer the different shipping costs to the buyer, you may affect the conversion rates negatively, and this will affect your profit margin. More importantly, it is not wise to pass the charges to your buyers.

There is a High Level of Competition

The dropshipping model is attractive that there are many people willing to engage in it. It has a high level of competition that often sends many startups into extinct. It is only easy to manipulate the competition if one is able to identify an extremely specialized niche.

It is Difficult to Track the Inventory

It is nearly impossible for you to keep track of your inventory. If you have all of your stock in a single store, you can easily trace their movement. However, having more than one supplier and warehouse where your products move from makes it difficult. The suppliers also deal with other merchants, and their inventory changes almost every day.

ECOMMERCE AND DROPSHIPPING

However, the introduction of certain apps can help to deal with it. You only need to sync with the suppliers. When you sync with the suppliers, you will be able to pass your orders to the suppliers and have access to the inventory they have. For instance, Oberlo makes it easier for a merchant to make automated decisions. If a supplier does not have a particular product anymore, the merchant can easily have the product un-published or set to zero quantity.

CHAPTER FIFTEEN

IS DROPSHIPPING FOR YOU?

Generally, all first-timer who want to go into e-commerce business can try out dropshipping. It is an attractive business model for anyone who does not have enough experience and too much to invest. You will experience low risk and low investment, and it makes it look less than a gamble. Also, a store owner who has a specific set of products but is interested in trying out other products can make use of the dropshipping model because it does not require much. Such investors can easily try out the new products and ascertain their demand before investing heavily in them and stocking them up. However, if you are interested in a large profit margin, the dropshipping model is not suitable for you. You may be disappointed. If you want to make profits at a higher level, you would have to approach manufacturers themselves, and the manufacturers do not usually offer to dropship. A new startup may also have challenges with dropshipping with the low-profit margin it offers. The brand is yet to get a hold on the control of its customer's satisfaction via branding and branding experience.

Nevertheless, there are certain categories of entrepreneur that will enjoy the dropshipping model. It will work well for them, and I have carefully selected them.

Entrepreneurs interested in Testing

Dropshipping is great for testing new products, the possibility of a new business growing successfully. You may need to test the possibility of your business making perfect sales before you invest in inventory. It is a business model for those who need validation before they make their investment, especially when the business requires a lot of capital.

Entrepreneurs on Budget

The dropshipping model is great for businesspersons who have limited resources in their domain. It is quite low in expenses and doesn't require high investment, hence any entrepreneur who wishes to make sales with as little as he or she can achieve his or her purpose with the dropshipping model.

New Entrepreneurs

If you are a newbie in the e-commerce business, dropshipping is a great option for your business. It is quite difficult to make sales online. You need to work hard to drive traffic to your website and make more efforts to make sure that your visitors become converted before you can successfully have an operating e-commerce store. With the low investment requirement that comes with dropshipping, a new entrepreneur will have enough time and resources to learn the methods of driving traffic and making the conversion that will aid sales before he or she starts to invest in stocks that will demand more of his or her time.

Entrepreneurs with Varieties of Interest

If you are an entrepreneur who wants to sell different products, dropshipping will work well for you. Especially if you don't have enough to stock the different products, you want to sell. With dropshipping, all you need is to get the orders and approach the suppliers to deliver the package to the customers. You don't have to buy the products you want to sell.

However, there are certain kinds of entrepreneurs that drop shipping will not augur well with. The model doesn't have a plan for them. Hence, for them to invest in it will greatly affect their businesses.

Brand-Centered Entrepreneurs

If you are a business person that loves to have a good image that will not be affected by any mistake in the course of the business, you may have challenges with dropshipping. It is quite hard and time-consuming to build a brand that is sustainable. Nonetheless, it gives a great reward. However, for you to build your brand with the dropshipping model is more difficult than you can think because there are a lot of factors of customer satisfaction that you are not in control of.

Aside from the point of getting orders and the payment, you do not have any contact with the customer anymore. The dropship supplier will take up the job from there.

Since it is the supplier that is in charge of the product delivery, you do not have control over the experience of the customer when he or she receives the package. Since you are not in charge of the shipping, most likely, the suppliers will not communicate your brand image to the buyers. Also, in a situation where is an issue with the delivery, you need to follow some long process with the dropship supplier to rectify the issue, and this may take a while, which will create a wrong impression about your brand to the customer. Building a solid brand with dropshipping is quite difficult to achieve.

Profit-Centered Entrepreneurs

If you are engrossed in making high profits, you are not liable for the dropshipping model. The dropshipping business models offer a razor-thin margin. Usually, an average drop shipping company makes a margin of 10 to 20%, which includes the price you sell a product minus the amount you pay the dropship supplier. Having deducted your credit card transaction fees, email service, and other management services, you would be left with little percent of the whole income. It is possible for your dropshipping business to make up to $1 million yearly in revenue, while the actual profit will be between $40,000 and $50,000 annually.

Marketers that Lack of Creativity

You need creativity to excel in the dropshipping business. The reason is that even the manufacturers of every product set goals to make up to 30% sales of their products through a direct-to-consumer model using their company's site. With this, if you plan to sell their products, you are obviously competing with them also. In a competitive game with this manufacturer, you have a lower chance of winning against them because they have the resources and a wider margin ahead of you. Therefore, winning will require you to be creative in your approach such that you will be able to identify new approaches that they will not think of to attract

ECOMMERCE AND DROPSHIPPING

your customers. This creativity should not end with Facebook Ads and Google Ads.

CHAPTER SIXTEEN

HOW TO START DROPSHIPPING

Starting a dropshipping business is similar to the process of starting any other e-commerce business model. There is a need for you to get yourself a marketable idea, a reliable source for your products, the medium through which you want to make your sales, and your marketing plans and strategies to help you build the business. The only area of divergence is the investment required, which is not high in the dropshipping business model. You don't have to gather a high amount before you can start your business. Also, you do not need facilities or employees. Your dropshipping business needs to have the following elements for it to be established and built up.

1. **A Dropshipping website/online store**
2. **Selection of the right and best products**
3. **Understanding your market**
4. **Identify the Best Suppliers**
5. **Grow Your Dropshipping Business**

In this chapter, I will look at the process of you building your dropshipping website, while the other elements will be discussed in subsequent chapters.

CREATING A DROPSHIPPING WEBSITE/ONLINE STORE

A dropshipping business is run from a website or an online store. This is what will put your business on the motion and get it to work out perfectly as you have wished. The online store is an e-commerce platform that will link you with the world. The next question is: How do I choose the right website or online store for my dropshipping business? Basically, there are two factors you need to consider to choose the best e-commerce platform for your business: the central idea of your business and the plan of your drop ship supplier. When these two elements combine together, you will be able to pick the best platform that works for you.

The Central Idea of Your Business

This answers the question of what the general focused of your business is? Are you primarily concerned about products or content? The need for thee is because there are certain eCommerce platforms that work well for content while some work well for products. If you are focusing on your product, Shopify will be a great option. An example of a dropship company utilizing Shopify is Goetz. The online business store is designed to function as a selling machine, without any blog or content section. It is designed to be a dropship-friendly platform. If you wish to build a website for your dropship business, which will also permit you to create content, you may go for WordPress.

Importance of Contents to Your Dropshipping Business

When you create content such as reviews, recipes, blog posts, etc., your website will have a high ranking in search engines, and this will drive more traffic to your online store. Also, it will be a boost to your marketing efforts. If you have a target of using content to your advantage, going for WordPress will be a great option. You can make use of Bluehost, which is a WordPress hosting service provider, and it works with WooCommerce, which is a common plugin for e-commerce. With Bluehost, you will get a free domain, free email address, an automatic set up of WooCommerce, and you will receive a free 2 hour set up a call, and everything costs you just $6.95 monthly.

The Plan of Your Dropship Supplier

There are many plug-and-play drop ship market platforms. Some popular ones that you may go for are Oberlo, Modalyst, Doba, Sprocket, etc. these four work well with Shopify. Hence, if you want to go for any of them, you are subscribing to Shopify. Shopify is great as it is leading when it comes to cutting-edge ship suppliers' integration. Shopify affords you the possibility of testing al available drop ship marketplaces, products, suppliers, and it makes it possible to be the first to carry out an experiment with new players as they are introduced. At present, Shopify supports up to 42

ECOMMERCE AND DROPSHIPPING

dropshipping marketplaces while it has full integration with Oberlo.

Another e-commerce platform you can go for is Volusion. It is fully integrated with a popular dropship marketplace – US Direct. With Volusion, you have the dashboard of the US Direct dropshipping marketplace with no need for any other installation. Volusion affords merchants using it the opportunity to access products of high quality from suppliers based in the USA. Also, as a seller, you can easily search many products for dropship across a wide range of categories, and you can just add them to your website with a single click.

These two platforms – Shopify and Volusion, make it easy for any new merchant to set up a dropshipping business faster than WordPress. However, the two platforms have limited content creation features. Having selected the platform, you need, you may have to carry out certain designs on the website to give it a special outlook. Your logo design is also important to make you stand out. For any of

ECOMMERCE AND DROPSHIPPING

these, you can always hire a freelancer who will help you do them at a cheap rate.

Note that you can also list some drop-ship items on popular and big marketplaces such s Walmart, Amazon, eBay, etc. however, you need should watch out always. These platforms have fees for sellers. They also have deadlines for their shipping, which are often strict, and they do set up customer service requirements. It is great to use these platforms. However, thy are not the best options for startups. You should first establish yourself and build your site. Learn the process from your site and then reach out to other seller marketplaces to expand.

CHAPTER SEVENTEEN

SELECTING THE BEST PRODUCT

Generally, the e-commerce business is all about the products you have to offer. How well are you able to select your products will go a long way in determining how well your business will fare. The dropshipping model requires you to select the best products that will deal with the needs of your customers. Whatever product you want to sell must have the general acceptance of your prospective customers. Remember, the more products you sell, the more successful your business will be. There is nothing as the "Perfect" product. However, there are products that are more suitable for the business to grow. You need certain criteria you must use to identify the best products you need to place on your online store. You can depend on figures, facts, and research to determine the varieties of products you need to sell. I have identified certain criteria you need to consider to select your products for dropshipping.

Retail price: you need to consider both the retail and wholesale prices of the products you want to sell. It is important for you to hit the sweet spot while you are pricing your product. When the price of the products is low, it will encourage the buyers to make purchases. However, you stand to have a low-profit margin on each product. However, products with high prices will give you a high-profit margin but low sales. In the prices of selecting your product, you need to identify what will work best for you and your customers. Consider the expectations of your customers and work toward it. The average profit margin for dropshipping is between 15% and 45%, and this should be the standard you want to work with. With this, you can price your products between $50 and $100, which is an optimal price; but you need to consider the product.

The Size and Weight of the Product: the price for packaging and shipping of products differ based on the cost of packaging the products with certain material, and the required effort to carry out the shipping of the products by workers or machine. To make the best and largest profit margin, you will have to go for products that have lighter weight and are very cheap to ship. You can also earn high by dropshipping products with a large profit margin; however, it is often advisable that you start small.

Check for Complementariness: Some products are best selected together. If you can identify such products that are related, you would be able to offer your customers the best value they require. This would motivate them to seek you more for their next purchases. You should look for products that you can sell together in a similar niche. For instance, easels will go well with other products such as paintbrushes, canvases, and other art supplies. You may decide to dropship it alongside other painting materials. While you select your products based on this, you need to strategically set the price of your products in such a way that it will meet up with the value of your buyers and yours. You can decide to sell your main item at a lower price, in order to motivate your customers to buy the item, while you make up for the loss by cross-selling the other related items to the item at a larger amount.

The Durability of the Product: you should consider the goods that will make your customers come back. Remember you online to make sales, not to write nor to influence. If you select products that are disposable or renewable, your customers will have little to no choice but come back to buy more, and this will increase your sales. You may set up a subscription model for your customers to always make them come back for purchases. To make the subscription works, you need to make it attractive by giving them a discount. This will make them sign up for it while they have to come back to repeat their orders.

Check out the Turn Over Rate of the Product: Another area you need to pay attention to is the rate of turnover of the products you want to sell. This rate refers to their level at which the products tend to change, get updated, or discounted, etc. You need to make sure that your products are not always changing in a short period of time. If they keep changing in a short time, you would have to keep creating new content, which requires your money and your time — thinking of the stress involved with the updating of the products also. You need to evaluate whatever product you plan to settle for so that you will not end up selecting products that will take more from you than what you would gain.

HOW YOU CAN FIND THE RIGHT PRODUCT FOR DROPSHIPPING

After you have followed these criteria, the next step you are left with is how to find the products you have selected. This involves you finding a place to source the products from. I have three steps you can take to get the preferred products that you want to dropship.

Create a List

You should set up a list (a Google Sheets will suffice), it should be a spreadsheet, which you would use to document the name and sources of the products you end up getting. This will save you from losing track of where you get the products from, and as well, it will serve as reference data for future references.

Search for Possible Sources

Don't ever make the mistake of forgetting the usefulness of Google in such a situation when you are stuck for an answer. You can search for the potential product you can dropship. There are lots of autocomplete suggestions that are common keywords, which many prospective customers often search for. With the Google search engine, you have access to many possible sources to get your products.

Check Forums and Review Sites: To identify the right products most of your people need, you can log into different websites and forums and check people's opinions and need for certain products. You will obviously see some clamoring for specific products; all you need to do is to get it and sell to them. With review sites, you will gain access to products that are ranking high among customers, and selling such will boost your sales. You may check popular reviews blogs such as AcquireMag, Uncrate, etc.

CHAPTER EIGHTEEN

UNDERSTANDING YOUR MARKET

Dropshipping business requires an understanding of how the market works. The working of the general e-commerce market may not be suitable for the dropshipping model because it deviates from the general principles of e-commerce. You, therefore, need to carry out a detailed analysis of your market to build your business on a solid foundation. To understand your market better, you should follow the following tips:

Measure the Demand Rate for Your Products: you can measure the demand rate for your products by using the KWFinder tool. The tool will reveal how the keywords for your products rank monthly. The ranking is based on the number of people that search for your product, and the result you get will let you know how well the product is in demand. Avoid starting out with a product. You are not sure of its demand, so you will not end up losing out.

Identify the Impact of Seasonal Changes on the Purchasing Altitude of Customers: there are;3certain products that are seasonal. However, some sell all through the year. You need to identify the effects of seasons on the purchasing habit of your customers. You should make use of Google Trends. Google Trends offers a graphical representational analysis of the zenith of searches for any product. When you have this fact, you will be able to make the right decision.

Analyze Your Competition: you should not fail to study your competition. Study their methods of engagement on the market. You should know your competitors well by searching through their websites, their social media outlets, and their presence on other major marketplaces like eBay and Amazon. Look at their ratings, their reviews, comments about their services, and how they engage with their customers. You are doing all these to identify the areas where your competitors are lagging behind, and you are utilizing the opportunity to your advantage.

Understanding Your Competition

For you to scale through your competitors, you need to understand the competition. Competition can be advantageous and dangerous. If there is an established seller for the product you want to sell, it is a great thing. It shows that the product has enough demands. However, when there are lots of buyers, the competition becomes dangerous since the market has perhaps become saturated. You are. Therefore, left with making decisions, nothing the presence of others. To make the right decisions that will stand you out despite your competition, you should take the following steps concerning the competition.

Learn about your competitors: You should never be in competition without knowing about your competitors. You can use SEMrush, an online website explorer that will help you identify the ranking of websites. You can even know the domain authority of your competitors. With this, you would know how much traffic they generate, how they are able to generate their traffic, and how their websites are faring. The knowledge will obviously aid you in making the best decisions for your business.

Check their Business Procedure: One way to do this by ordering a product from your competitor. You would get to know how they operate, their customer service. You will get to see the difference between their online presence and their physical dealing with customers if there is any. You would get to see the best of them, and the worst part of them, which is where you need to work on to be unique. You may also pick ideas from their best parts; however, do not copy them.

Study their Social Media Platforms: you will get to know about the feelings of their customers through their social media platforms. From there, you would get their market strategy and know where you need to work on. Remember that as it is in the e-commerce business, customer service and support are also important to dropshipping business. Whatever flaws you observe should be your area of strength. Study their content, and see the way it generates leads for them. You can then pattern your content in the direction.

FACTORS YOU SHOULD CONSIDER ABOUT YOUR TARGET MARKET

There are some factors you need to consider while you set your target market. Your target market is the specific set or category of customers you plan to sell to. If you want to select the target market, you need to look out for certain factors in them, such as the following:

Demographics: Demographics has to do with the location, the income of the customers you want to target. You need to know this to know how big your audience is, where they are. This piece of information will guide you on how well you can drop ship your products to them excellently.

Gender: You need to select the gender you want. And if you want both genders, you can make the decision. However, studies have revealed that male and female genders have different spending and purchasing patterns. You will have to look into what motivates the gender to buyer, what kind of content will work well with the gender, and the device the gender uses to buy. You should also check out for the specific form of language that will effectively convert them.

Age: You need to identify the age bracket of the customers you want to target. There are separate patterns of purchase for different age groups. Studies revealed that those born between 1980 and 2000 tend to spend less, and they earn less. As a result, it would be a bad idea to dropship products that are expensive to people within the age bracket. Also, those above 60 years do not take delight in internet shopping.

The Institution: You need to identify the specific institution you plan to sell to. Are you selling to individuals, businesses, or government? There are different forms of the e-commerce business. Are you into business 2Busines, Business 2 consumer, or Business 2 Government? This knowledge will show you who you are really dealing with within the business as your consumers.

CHAPTER NINETEEN

IDENTIFY THE BEST SUPPLIERS

The success of a dropshipping business lies in the functionality of the suppliers. If you want to build a successful dropshipping business, you need to find the appropriate suppliers who will work efficiently and punctually. You are only responsible for the virtual aspect of the business; however, your supplier handles the physical aspect, which is more important than the virtual aspect that you handle. If you successfully create an attractive online store that generates much traffic and gives you lots of conversions, but your supplier messes up when it is time to deliver, you would lose all of your resources and hard work because customers do not want to patronize a business they had an unimpressive experience with at first. You need a supplier that can stick to the specific form of the image you have tried to create online with the customers.

When you choose your supplier, you have to consider some features and factors so you will not select wrongly.

Select an Experienced Dropship Supplier that has Supportive Sales Representative: you need to make your selection based on experience. It is often better to select a drop shipper that is experienced in the business. Such a person understands the challenges that relate to the dropshipping business and will know how best to handle them. The supplier should also have a sales representative that will be around to answer your queries and create a great communication line with you.

Select a Dropshipper that offers Quality products: when you give products with high quality, you will earn the satisfaction of your customer. When your customers love the delivery, there will be a reduction in the rate at which products will be returned. And there will be better customer reviews, which will build the business by drawing others to buy from you. Hence, quality product I an important prerequisite for any supplier you want to select.

Select based on Technological Know-how: the supplier you want to choose must have technological abilities to relate well with times. In the process of growth, you should be able to retain your drop shipper and not let him or her go because he or she does not have the technological capabilities to bear with your growth requires.

Select based on Efficiency and Punctuality with Shipping Procedure: Make sure the supplier you are selecting has a track record of efficiency and punctuality with the process of shipping. You can search for a drop shipper that delivers products within 24 to 48 hours. This way, you will be having great reviews from your customers since they would be happy. You can place a test order to your supplier to check out how he or she works. This will inform you about the supplier's tardiness if there is any.

ECOMMERCE AND DROPSHIPPING

SEARCHING FOR A SUPPLIER

Google is also a trusted friend in this respect. There are lots of startups and websites that are into e-commerce. When you research, you will see these businesses, and they often have the complete directories of dropship suppliers, with their contact information. You can select your choice of drop shipper through these contact lists, and send them an email based on some inquiries. The question you ask them is tactical. You are trying to check out their rate of response, and how helpful their sales representatives are. You need to vet the supplier you plan to work with. This will not always give you the perfect result you need. However, it will be effective to help you access to some degree the feasibility of both you and the supplier to work together. In the email you want to send, you can include some of the following questions.

Do you produce customized items if a person requires it?

What are the terms of your pricing, and can a person negotiate?

ECOMMERCE AND DROPSHIPPING

Will I have to pay for another cost aside from the direct costs? You need to be sure that no other cost is attached.

Does your company offer a return policy?

D-o, you also engage in direct selling or retailing?

What is the profit margin I should expect from working with you?

Do your prices fluctuate?

Will the product have a warranty coverage?

Is there a customer care representative that will always attend to me?

Do you make use of a data feed?

With these questions, the supplier will not be able to take advantage of you. It shows you know what you are doing and that you have full detail of the business. Don't let the supplier take you less seriously because you are s starter. There is a level of commitment both parties need to show to the retailer-supplier relationship.

Dealing with Dropshipping Scams

You are likely to come across many dropship scams in the business. You have to safeguard yourself and the business against them. There are certain signals you need to watch out for, such as an instance when a drop shipper rejects checks or credit, but requests for bank transfer as the only means of payment. This is a signal that you should beware of. Also, scams will not use an address on their business correspondence or websites. Every legal supplier is expected to display his or her address. Also, scams often adopt a method of age-old membership fees. At times, it may not be a scam; however, you need to carry out research to know its authenticity. Below are certain measures you can take to protect yourself from the scams.

Check the age of the domain using online tools: This is a great way to check the truth behind the claims of the supplier you meet. If the domain is new, beware it could be a scam. By checking the age of the domain, you will get to know the experience level of the supplier even if the supplier is not a scam; you can still make your decisions based on what you find out.

Read the Reviews about the Supplier: You can rely on people's words sometimes concerning others. If the supplier had scammed someone before, you would get to know if you go online to read reviews about the supplier. The person would have complained and left a warning message against the further occurrence.

Legally established Supplier: make sure the supplier is registered, and the supplier's warehouse or office should be located in an environment of commercial activities. If the office/warehouse address is showing a residential area, it is a signal that the supplier might be a scam.

Finding the right supplier is not that difficult. You only need to take the right steps. Ask the right questions, take the appropriate steps, carry out your research. You need to work with the right supplier to build your business and excel at it.

CHAPTER TWENTY

GROW YOUR DROPSHIPPING BUSINESS

You are welcome to the last stage of setting up your dropshipping business, which is for you to grow it from scratch to a state of success. You have done researches, identified the right products, met the right drop shipper, created the online store, and now, it is time for you to make the business grow. Every step I mentioned above is just a phase of the dropshipping business that you must pass through. You need to pass through the second phase, which has to do with you marketing your business and products. The best way to grow your dropshipping business is to market it. How well can you present your business to others? How much do people know about your product? These questions show how well your business is faring.

In marketing your products and business, you should be able to ask yourself the question: how will I sell my products if there is no one that knows my products? Why should my business and brand be trusted? Marketing will provide answers to these questions. A visitor coming to your website for the first time should be able to trust your brand. There are lots of strategies you can utilize to market your dropshipping business. If you follow a strategy adequately, it will work out well for you, and you would enjoy the result as time passes. I have identified five tools you can use to build your dropshipping business. These tools are; Social media, Customer reviews, email marketing, and Pay per clicks advertising.

#Tool 1 – Social Media

Generally, social media is a great platform for the marketing of e-commerce businesses. It is great for creating and distributing content. There are lots of people on social media, with daily interactions. Facebook, as an example, has over 1 billion active users. There are different social media strategies you can make use of to grow your dropshipping business. These strategies are meant to drive traffic to your website. You will be able to reach the targeted audience for your business and convert them so they can shop with you. With social media, you can easily build an engaged audience. However, social media requires your resources and time. This is why you need a strategy that will work well with your business. To create your social media strategy, you should follow the following frameworks:

#1 – Have your goals in mind. Whatever social media content you want to create should be geared toward a specific purpose. Are you trying to get comments, likes, interaction, etc.? Whatever it is that you want to get should be clearly stated out. The goals will help you identify the type of outcome you want to see at the end of social media usage. Widen your reach. Getting your brand in front of more people increases the chances of the right people seeing your brand. Your goals should revolve around the need to get more people interested in your products, increasing your mail list, having proof from readers though their comments, being able to get back to your customers through the medium, driving more traffic to your website, creating an

engaging environment with your audience, and finally, increasing your sales.

#2 – *Work with your target audience.* You should have a specific category of people in mind that you want to relate the content on your social media platforms too. When you know them, identify what motivates them and work toward that. The social media is filled with a crowd, and they are not all for you and your business; however, among the crowd, you have your audience that you need to identify. You should use the demographics mentioned earlier as a guideline.

#3 – *Get the right content.* Your content must be captivating for people to want to stay and read. Your content must blend with your goals, and the type of audience you are targeting. Your content might be news, entertainment, inspirational, question and answers, promotional contents, etc. most importantly, your content should always add value to your audience. make them await your next post for what they know they would gain. And have a consistent schedule on how you post.

#4 – Select your channel. You should have a specific channel you want to be known for. avoid being a Jack of all trade. Have a specific platform where you make a wave. When you have more than one channel, you would have to maintain them all, and it may become cumbersome. At the start of your business, it is advisable that you focus on 1 or 2 platforms, so you will be able to monitor it or them. You can later have many platforms when your business has grown, and you can afford to enlist the skill of social media managers for each of the platforms.

#5 – Create a procedure. Don't just run social media without a process. There should be schedules and plans for every activity that goes on the platform. Have time for posting and well-grounded management of the social media platform. Make everything organized.

#6 – Be prone to changes. You should revolve with social media and make your procedure change also. By using social media analytics data, you will be able to follow every new stride on social media. You only need to make changes that

ECOMMERCE AND DROPSHIPPING

will suit it. Watch out for trends and make your platforms work inline with them.

#Tool 2 – Customer's Reviews

Customer reviews are a great tool in e-commerce and dropshipping business. No customer has the opportunity of meeting you; so, you can't explain your services and products enough. You need the rating of buyers who already purchased the product from you. The reviews customers give can either destroy or build a business. Other customers would trust the words of another customer who had used your products than your description of the products. To get the best customer's reviews, you need to give your customers the best experience they had ever wished for. your ability to make sure that they get exactly what they had paid for, will earn you their loyalty, which they will later affirm on your website. There are ways for you to have reviews on your website to make more sales. Follow these steps and experience a soar in the growth of your dropshipping business.

- You can ask your customers to give you feedback in the form of reviews on your service. This is the best way to get reviews. Usually, 70% of customers tend to leave behind reviews when the seller requests them. You may send them an email requesting it or have n app that automatically requests them to do so.
- You can make use of incentives to make your customers leave reviews. You will only have to reward them for the reviews. The reward can come in the form of a discount or small gift.
- You should make use of photo reviews. You can ask a customer to give you permission to place his or her photo on your site with the product you deliver to him or her. This will create a kind of trust in the minds of others who are willing to buy from you.
- Stay away from fake reviews. Your reviews are geared toward building your brand, and one important ingredient is trust. You are able to build trust matters. You should stay off from whatever will tarnish your image. You should start building your reviews when you get people.
- You can borrow reviews from other websites that sell similar products as yours. You may borrow from AliExpress. The customer will not mention your brand, but the product will be reviewed.
- Make it easy for people to leave reviews on your website. There are apps that permit you to write your review in your email, and it will be posted on your site automatically. With this, the customers will find it easy to write reviews about the products.

#Tool 3 – Email Marketing

Emails marketing is the least explored tools for building businesses. Many people even think they would become a nuisance for sending emails to their customers from time to time. Email marketing is a great tool for keeping your customers abreast of your products and business. When there are price changes, discounts, new product-related content, etc., you can easily keep your customers updated by sending them emails. Email marketing is one great way of bringing your first-time buyers back to yourself. To have easy email marketing, you should do the following:

- Create an email list. There should be a list of people who had either patronized you once or more. you should, however, pay close attention to the most loyal customers (I hope you still remember the Paleto principle of 80/20?)
- Utilize different email marketing practices. There are lots of purposes that an email can be used to achieve. It all depends on the behavior of the buyers that you need to correct. One such attitude is leaving the cart behind. You can send an email to remind a buyer who abandoned his or her cart. Some customers just pick goods but end up leaving the goods without buying. The email you send may change such a

person's mind. The email will be targeted at encouraging the customer to finish his or her order. There are other email marketing practices, such as up-sell and cross-sell emails. These are often used to offer a buyer who already bought some items more items. And there are promotional emails, which are used to inform customers about new products, or a reduction/ increase in price, etc.
- You need to compose good emails with an outstanding subject that will catch the attention of your customers.
- You should also schedule your email. Tuesdays, Wednesdays, and Thursdays are the most advisable days for email marketing for any purpose. You should, however, be careful of Tuesdays and Thursdays because people tend to receive more emails.

#Tool 4 – Pay Per Click Advertising

The PPC Ads are a form of advertisement that makes an advertiser pay each time a customer clicks on an ad that the advertiser had created to generate people to his or her website. PPC ads are not cheap; however, it helps with the increasing of a person's conversion. There is a need to monitor a pay per click ads so that it will not only generate traffic without getting them to buy. The intention is to bring them and convert them. In the process of creating a PPC ad, you need to understand the industry very well and select the right keywords. Your content should motivate people to click on the advert, and there is a need for a landing page that will help you to convert the people who click the ads. Many social media platforms give room for PPC adverts. Among the popular ones are Facebook Ads and Google Ads.

CHAPTER TWENTY-ONE

DEALING WITH DROPSHIPPING MISTAKES

There are lots of mistakes and challenges that surround the drop ship business. There is a lot of information online and offline, and many people tend to get their advice from various angles. However, some of these pieces of advice do not state deeply what most startups need to do appropriately. This often leads to mistakes that could have been avoided by the newbies. Although the dropshipping business has a wide range of benefits to offer, it is also embedded with certain setbacks and unwanted events, which may lead to a struggle with the business.

DROPSHIP COMMON MISTAKES

I have identified five common mistakes that most sellers make in the dropship business, and I have highlighted the best way to deal with each of these mistakes. You should know these mistakes so that you would be able to avoid such when next you are about to go into your business, or if you are already in your business, you just check out whether any of these mistakes is what you are guilty of, and make the appropriate corrections to the mistake.

Lack of Specialization (Niche)

This is the easiest and commonest mistakes many dropship sellers make. When you try to offer different varieties of products based on the easiness that comes with dropshipping, you are placing yourself and your business into a pit. Well, it is quite great for you to offer varieties for your customers; however, you need to monitor it so that it won't grow out of hand. Make sure that what you offer is not too wide that you won't be able to monitor it. When a business is not focused and does not work with a specific target audience in mind, it will become difficult for such businesses to grow and attract customers.

How to Deal with it

You should carry out research on the niche that would develop your business. Create a brand specifically for the niche you are going for and be known for that niche. You should have a certain category of products you want to sell to people. Let people know you for that particular product, and you would be considered an expert at it in no time. This will create loyalty from your customers toward you, and you will experience an increase in your sales.

Lack of a Business Plan

Many startups are easily carried away with the need to identify the product to sell. The automated and user-friendly platforms for starters are also contributing factors to this mistake. Most people just go into the setting up of their business and start thinking about how to make sales. You may sell the product; however, with the easiness you get to sell the product, you can easily fold up the business as well. The mistake here is that you do no start selling without a strategy – business plan. You should have a procedure and guidelines that will help you achieve more than working blindly.

How to Deal with it

You are expected to carry out research before you start your business. There should be a plan for the kinds of products you want to dropship, the suppliers you want to use, and how the business operations will be like. You must also stick to these strategies.

Lack of Connection Between Your Strategy and Dropshipping

Many e-commerce sellers who wish to include the dropshipping model into their businesses often encounter issues. The problem often comes up with their inability to create a synergy between their existing business strategy and drop shipping, which. They are about adding. You must be sure that dropshipping fits in well into your business before you try to connect them together. For instance, if you have a marketing strategy that relies on branding and customization, you will encounter a great challenge with dropshipping because in dropshipping, you will not be touching most of the products being delivered.

How to Deal with it

Identify the effects that dropshipping would have on your business, and look out for how it will impact your customer's experience. Check if you would find an alternative means to dropship. If drop shipping stops you from adding branding to your packaging, you can just make use of email marketing, messages, and any other means you can take to engage your customers.

Lack of Customer Support After Sale

Many sellers believe since they are not in charge of the product's delivery, they can look away from what happens next after the customer pays. Hence, many of them end their interaction with their customers once the customer placed their orders. Nonetheless, it is vital that you have a customer support system that will keep interacting with your customers even after the sale. This engagement is even more important for those dealing in dropshipping. Your suppliers are prone to make mistakes. The earlier you understand this, the better it is for your business. In such instances, you need to be able to deal with the situation through a platform where the customers can come back to relate with you. Customers don't know whether you are dropshipping or you don't. All they see is you and your brand, and they want YOU to deliver their goods to them a soon as possible.

How to Deal with it

You should be available to deal with customer care issues as soon as possible. Whenever an issue arises, you should never blame anyone for the mistake, just let your customers know that you have plans to fix the problem. Be in touch with your customers after they had placed their orders. You may use a thank you email to keep in touch.

Lack of Right Suppliers

Suppliers are the life wire of the drop ship business. Even when you had labored, and placed efforts into building a brand for yourself, if you fail to get the right suppliers, you are just going to jeopardize your business. The market is filled with lots of suppliers – both good and bad. You need to pick the best suppliers to give your business a good outlook.

How to Deal with this

Don't just pick any supplier. You need to carry out your research on the suppliers you plan to work with. You should read different reviews about the various suppliers through websites, ask about them from other sellers who are into business with them. Your choice of the supplier should be someone you can contact on the phone, and see to it that the supplier has a customer care representative that you can speak with to address any issues. When a supplier breaks your trust, you should not have any reason to stick to him or her.

You can avoid these mistakes by planning your business and reviewing every activity that goes on in the business. You need to diligently give your all to make sure that you give your customers the best satisfaction they deserve. Dropshipping is viable for you to earn a living in the e-commerce business.

ECOMMERCE AND DROPSHIPPING

CHAPTER TWENTY-TWO

DEALING WITH DROPSHIPPING CHALLENGES

The popularity of the dropshipping business model has not subsidized. Rather, people keep showing interest in the business. Dropshipping is a model that gives e-commerce traders the opportunity to expand their business with little or no extra capital. These have garnered a lot of responses from people who had shown interest in the business. The business allows you to sell as much as possible products without investing in stocking any of them. However, just as life itself is not always rosy, the dropshipping business also has its shortcomings. All businesses have their area of lacking where every businessperson needs to make adjustments and work in line with. There are certain challenges or problems, as you may like to address them, that come with the dropshipping business. Having an understanding of these problems now will go a long way to help you deal with them when you encounter any of them later. I have identified five common challenges you should expect in your dropshipping business.

#Challenge 1 – Identifying the Right Supplier

Suppliers are one of the backbones of the dropshipping business model. To be successful at it, you must find yourself a trustworthy supplier. There are lots of people acting as suppliers who are actually not. You need to make your findings and make sure that you get the best one. The challenge with suppliers is that they represent you to the customers, and when they fail to deliver well, your customers will not blame them; it is your brand that will bear the burnt (Go through chapter nineteen to see how you can choose the right supplier).

#Challenge 2 – Lack of Stock

Items that are popular usually run out of stock, and this, at times, leads to a bad customer relationship. When customers come online to search for a product and discover that it is not available, that will give them a wrong impression about your business, especially when that will be the customer's first attempt to buy from you. Customers don't understand that you are not in charge of the product. They only see you. Hence, to deal with this, you should more than one supplier that sells the same product. If a supplier runs out of stock, you should have another supplier to fall back on. You may also make arrangements for substitute items, and send it to the customer, while you update the customer.

#Challenge 3 – Having more Sales

There is a high level of competition in the market. The market is kind of saturated already, and to make an impact in it would require a lot from you. There are others who made the right choice from the start. They had the right suppliers, and they often get profitable products to dropship. However, they have a challenge with getting customers to their stores.

There is a need for them to create a strategy that will help them drive traffic to their website and convert as many people as possible.

You should adopt a similar strategy used to promote online business. Blogging, email marketing, writing an eBook, SEOs, and creating podcasts will be of help. You only have to look out for the best options that will work for you.

#Challenge 4 – Customer's Dissatisfaction with a Product

Customers can show dissatisfaction with a package based on the claim that the product you deliver is bad. You may deliver a product that is below the expectation of the customer, or probably the supplier failed to provide the right description of the product, which the buyer read before ordering. When this happens, you need to look for a way to apologize for the inconveniences you might have caused the customer. Ask questions on why the customer considers the product has been bad and be polite about it. Let the customer see that you are willing to get feedback to improve your business and future deals with others. With this, you would have prevented a possible occurrence of the situation in the future.

#Challenge 5 – Bad reviews on Social media

Customers act as town criers to businesses. Whether they enjoy your services or detest it, they will help to amplify their experiences online. Social media is a place where anyone can easily express his or her mind. Many businesses face the challenge of their customers going to social media to rant about their displeased service. You may have a similar situation in the course of running your business. It is not every customer that has the patience to calm down and seek redress from you when he or she is displeased at your service and product.

This situation places the reputation of a person at stake. You always need to provide answers to people's complaints online. If you keep mute, others will see it as you not caring about the need of your customers, while those who read the reviews will have no trust in your credibility. However, if you can respond to their complaints, and acknowledge your mistakes, people would see your sincerity and trust you. Don't run from the situation; rather, make the situation right.

There are lots of challenges that come with the dropshipping business. However, you can always overcome them by taking the right steps to deal with them. The first step is to be aware of them, which you are by now. Then, take the necessary steps you think will help to mitigate the effect of the challenges that cannot be totally avoided.

PART THREE

PROVIDING NEEDFUL ANSWERS

007
CHAPTER TWENTY-THREE

QUESTIONS ON E-COMMERCE

I have some questions that you may probably have concerning e-commerce business generally. In this chapter, my intention is to leave you without/ with fewer questions to ask. This chapter will answer questions that the part on e-commerce in this book didn't fully cover.

Question: Who are those that can sell online?
Answer: Well, the online space looks as if it is for a group of people. However, it is not so. Anybody can sell online. That is, e-commerce is for everyone; however, not everyone is fit to sell online. There some factors you need to consider before you start an online business. You should look into

what you can sell online. The knowledge of what will sell online will reveal to you who can sell online. E-commerce is for both services and products. Hence, if you provide services or sell products that people need, then you can sell online. The key to selling online is to have valuable goods that people need.

Question: How much does a person need to start an e-commerce business?

Answer: The amount you need to start selling online is little when compared to what you need to sell in a physical shop. There are two methods to selling online: you either create an e-commerce website, or you sell your products through other platforms, such as eBay, Amazon, etc. The amount you need to start selling depends greatly on which method you want to apply, and the kind of product you plan to sell. If you are creating your website to sell, you need to get funds for the following: your website design, internet connection, and the cost of you providing the product or service. While if you are selling on another's platform, your expenses include: internet connection, the cost of providing the product.

ECOMMERCE AND DROPSHIPPING

Question: What is the percentage of profit I can make on each online sale?

Answer: There is no fixed percentage of profit that you can make as you sell online. Many factors determine your online sales, and these factors are peculiar to each business. There is only assurance I can give: you would most probably get a higher percentage of profit on a product sold online than the similar product sold physically. The reason is that you spend less to provide the product online.

Question: Do the size of my product and my customer database have a limit online?

Answer: You don't have any limit to the size of your product and the database you can get from your customers. E-commerce affords you the opportunity to add unlimited products, and you can always increase the database of your customers.

Question: Will my business start making sales immediately? Did I set up my account?

Answer: Your business is not expected to start making sales immediately. You need to drive traffic to your website and get people to show interest in wanting to buy from you. You need to develop a special selling proposition that will sell your products. There are lots of competitions in e-commerce. Hence, you must first market your business and product to start selling.

Question: What is the F-Strategy all about?

Answer: the 3 F strategy is to combat the slow rate of loading of many websites pages, which often send customers away from their store. The websites are also cluttered, with complex navigation that requires apt understanding by visitors to be able to move from one part of the site to another. The 3F strategy is to make your website *Fast, Functional, and Familiar.* When people come to your website, they want to buy from you. However, you need to be available to assist them in making their orders as quickly as possible. When your prospective customers don't get the user-friendly interface they seek, they would leave the page, and not complete their order. I will explain the three Fs in brief.

Fast: you must make sure that the website is well built to be fast. Your hosting, email responses, the loading speed of your site, the processing of orders, and paying, all of these should be fast and not drag the buyers down. The loading speed of your site should be a maximum of 5 seconds.

Functional: your website should be functional. You need to ascertain the specific goal you want your website to accomplish. Let your customers have access to your products and get what they actually want and need. If you fail to provide them with what they want, they will look elsewhere.

Familiar: Your customers need to be comfortable with your website. Use an easy navigation method that will make it fun and attractive for customers to stay online with you and make purchases. There should be a clear structure and layout of your pages, have common navigation buttons, make your text clear, etc

CHAPTER TWENTY-FOUR

QUESTIONS ON DROPSHIPPING

This chapter contains some useful answers to some questions that you may not get to understand directly and fully by reading the on dropshipping alone. These questions will explain further the effectiveness of the dropshipping business model to you as an e-commerce investor.

Question: To what extent is Dropshipping viable and profitable?

Answer: Generally, dropshipping has a profit margin that ranges between 15% and 45%. But certain items, such as durable goods and luxury items for consumers, can give up to 100% profit margin. You only need to identify the best niche and the right suppliers. One way for you to earn a high margin of profit is for you to get your products directly for the manufacturer rather than the supplier/wholesaler. This could have helped you do away with the middle man. You can make your first $1millionsales in a year the same year you opened your online store. However, this happens less.

Question: Is there any difference between a dropshipping manufacturer, wholesaler, and an aggregator?

Answer: Yes, they are all different. But, people use them interchangeably in the e-commerce business. A manufacturer is the producer of the products a seller sells online. It is possible for the manufacturer to have a drop ship program or not. However, it is best for the retailer if the manufacturer has a dropship program because that will enable the retailer to buy directly from them.

The dropshipping wholesaler is also the supplier, usually. They buy the products from the manufacturer in large quantities and help to deliver them to the buyers of the retailers.

A drop ship aggregator is different. It refers to a person that buys various kinds of products from many producers to offer the retailer a large variety of products he or she can sell. The

ECOMMERCE AND DROPSHIPPING

aggregator helps to resolve many of the challenges that may face a retailer during the running of his or her business. It helps to reduce shipping costs to many suppliers, and it prevents the waste of time trying to send out orders in multiples to lots of vendors. However, aggregators demand high pay from the profit, and this can affect the expectation of the retailer.

Question: How much do I need to start a dropshipping business?

Answer: The response to this is determined by what you want. That is your preference. No one can really give an exact amount. However, there are certain things you need to spend on to start. These things are compulsory and don't change. You can take these as the most important costs you must make. *Your online store (at $29 monthly)*. It is great to use a Shopify store for your online store. It will enable you to sync with Oberlo, which is a marketplace that will help you to source products, and give you access to the various themes selections and branding kits you may want to use. *Your Domain name (at $5 to $20 annually). Your test orders* *(this varies on the product you want to test by ordering it to check for any defects or shortcomings on the part of the suppliers). Your online Ads (You may budget $500 as a starter).* These are the basic expense you need to cater for as you start your dropshipping business.

Question: How do I make money as a dropship retailer?

Answer: The dropshipping business is a form of curator for products. It helps to select different products and get them to the reach of the customers to make the order for them. Since you are helping customers to identify, evaluate, and buy the product they really need, you will be charging them, by including the cost of customer support, on whatever product they order. Your drop shipping business will drive an additional sale to every supplier you work with. Hence, to make your profit, you need to find out the actual cost of getting a customer, and when you set the price on the product, that will be part of the factors you consider.

Question: Is dropshipping legalized?

Answer: Yes, the business is legalized. It has gained a wide range of acceptance from global e-commerce retailers.

ECOMMERCE AND DROPSHIPPING

Although the retailers are not selling their products, however, with the support of the manufacturer, they can sell the product by working with suppliers. However, you need to take some steps to make your business go legal. You will have to meet with an attorney whose specialty is in business matters to help you run your business legally in your area.

Questions: How do I handle a refund, return, and replacement of my Drop shipped items?

Answer: You cannot escape the need to refund a customer, or replace a Dropshipped item back to a customer. It is part of how online businesses are run. You cannot achieve a 100% customer satisfaction rate. You only need to make sure that the dissatisfaction rate is highly reduced. There is a process of refunding a returned Dropshipped product. They are as follows:

- The dissatisfied customer will place a return order and seek a refund through mail or phone.
- You will ask the supplier to give you a return merchandise authorization number
- Once the product gets back to the supplier from the customer, the supplier will refund the product money

back to you, and you would refund the full payment made back to the customer.

There is a return policy, and usually, a timeframe is often set. If the customer is asking for a refund within that timeframe, you need to undergo the tedious process and refund the customer.

Question: what if the supplier is at fault for the return of the product?

Answer: If the customer is returning the product as a result of the failure of the supplier to deliver the right product, the supplier will be willing to either replace the product without charges or reimburse the customer. Also, you need to have a stated agreement with the supplier on issues like this.

Questions: How do I handle inventory?

Answer: although the dropshipping business does not involve the retailer being in charge of a personal inventory, there may still be a need for you to maintain inventory. In this case, when your inventory order is not directly taken to the dropshipping suppliers, you need to manage the inventory orders. There are apps that will help you with this.

ECOMMERCE AND DROPSHIPPING

Question: What is the prospect for dropshipping in 2020?

Answer: There are great prospects for the business beyond the year 2020. Generally, e-commerce businesses will continue to rise, and dropshipping being a model of e-commerce will also benefit from this. As long as people are interested in buying, there will always be space for you in the business. However, you need to know that business is not perfect. Don't see it as a stress-free method of making millions online. You must be diligent in making money from dropshipping. Despite the benefits that come with dropshipping, there are complexities you need to address. Once all these complexities are resolved, you are prepared for success in the future. The tips on how to deal with drop shipping mistakes and risks will be helpful for you to deal with the complexities.

CONCLUSION

THE FUTURE OF DROP SHIPPING AND YOU

For every businessperson I have heard talked about business, they always talk about the need to be able to project into the future. Truly, there is a need for you as an investor to have a great *Foresight* to see into the future and know whether to take a specific decision or not. And also, you need to have an impressive *Hindsight* that will help you look into the past and bring out the best from it. In a research report by Forrester some years ago, it was reported that the e-commerce business would increase in size to $370 billion by the end of the year 2017. Most importantly, 23% of this growth would come from dropshipping businesses, which is equivalent to $85.1 billion. In 2019, it was estimated that the sales from e-commerce would account for 13.7% of the total retail sales globally., and by 2021, it would have grown to

ECOMMERCE AND DROPSHIPPING

17.5% sales of the overall sales. This is a show of the consistent rise that the e-commerce business tends to experience.

With this knowledge, one needs not to be deceived that investing in e-commerce, and the dropshipping model, especially, is a good way of making a fortune in the coming years. Dropshipping is not really an opened business that everyone understands how it works. The reason is that most customers do not care about the process of getting their products. They only want to see what they need and place an order for it while it comes to them. All you need is to create a good reputation for yourself and be engaged with your customers to always come back to you. For you, as a retailer, you will be creating a great future for yourself by investing in the dropshipping business for the following reasons:

The Sourcing of product: you don't have an issue with getting the product. Unlike the conventional method of selling that requires you to have a physical warehouse and to get your products from different wholesalers before you can sell, dropshipping allows you to sell a wider variety of products without you sourcing any of them into a warehouse. You can even deal with the producer without any middleman. All you have is a store that you maintain. The wholesaler or supplier maintains the products until you find a buyer who comes and places an order.

Storing of items: Dropshipping does not require you to create a store where you pack your products. The products do not stay with you. They are with the suppliers until they are purchased. This shows that you have less to lose but more to gain.

The fulfillment of order: There has always been a lack of interest by many e-commerce sellers to pack and arrange for the shipping orders they get. So, they end up giving out their orders to other establishments such as Amazon FBA, to help them fulfill. However, dropshipping makes it easy for you to fulfill an order. You only need to inform the suppliers, and they will carry it out.

You can achieve a high rate of Scalability: you can sell a high rate of the product beyond what you can afford as an investor. An example is Wayfair, one of the leading dropshipping retailers. The company drops ships more than 8 million products from 10,000 wholesalers and suppliers. This is quite possible because you are an only concern with marketing and the need to bring the customers. You don't have limitations to the amount of product you can offer based on what you have in store or what you don't have. You can always get from a large number of suppliers.

You have little to nothing to fear as a dropship retailer. Your side of the investment is quite low compared to following the conventional online business. Your future with the future of the dropshipping business tends to shine brighter than you may even think. Make a decision today and begin to build an empire of wealth from e-commerce.

www.ingramcontent.com/pod-product-compliance
Lightning Source LLC
Chambersburg PA
CBHW070631220526
45466CB00001B/152